Questions
and
Answers
on
Club Law

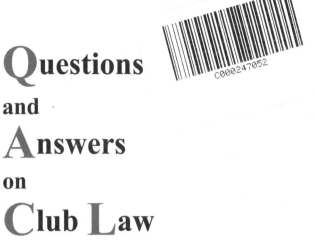

Peter Coulson LL.B

Benedict Books
© 2002

First published 1986 by Benedict Book Limited
Second edition 2002

© 2002 Peter Coulson

Published 2002 by: Benedict Books
　　　　　　　　　PO Box 900
　　　　　　　　　Hemel Hempstead
　　　　　　　　　Herts HP3 0RJ

Printed and bound in Great Britain by:
　　　　　　　　　MPG Books Ltd, Bodmin, Cornwall

Set in 9/10 Times New Roman

ISBN 1 870042 026

Introduction

T he law which governs clubs is complex, as never before. This book is an attempt to give guidance on a wide variety of issues which affect clubs in their daily activities, both with members and with outsiders.

The questions which you will find here may be familiar to you. That is because every one of them results from a letter, telephone call or email which I have had from a club official asking me to explain the law, as simply as I can, so that they can take suitable and appropriate action.

I am conscious that most club officials are amateurs — giving their time often without payment of any kind, in order to ensure that their club runs smoothly and within the law. My job, as it has been for over 30 years now, is to distil the innumerable Acts of Parliament, rules and regulations into something which can be understood by the layman, but which is as accurate and reliable as I can make it in the context of a club official's legal responsibilities.

The first edition of this book has been consistently popular for those very reasons. This second edition is long overdue, and it brings everything up to date, as far as is possible in an ever-changing world, where the law is altered even before the ink is dry!

The law in this book is accurate, as far as I can evaluate, to June 2002. Readers should be aware that fees, fines and other fiscal elements are at the whim of Chancellors, departments and others, which is why for the most part they have been avoided, for you to make your own current enquiries. As ever, I can be contacted through the publishers if you wish to ask a particular question. Otherwise, I wish your club every possible success.

Peter Coulson
June 2002

By the same author: The Law and You (Liquor licensing)
Successful Club Management (ed.)

To M.J.R.

Guide to questions

Chapter 1 - Club formation and constitution

Chapter 2 - Trustees and club property

Chapter 3 - Club finance and accounts

Chapter 4 - Club rules

Chapter 5 - Membership and subscriptions

Chapter 6 - Officers and their duties

Chapter 7 - The committee

Chapter 8 - Elections and nominations

Chapter 9 - Meetings and voting

Chapter 10 - Members' rights and obligations

Chapter 11 - The courts and the police

Chapter 12 - Running the bar

Chapter 13 - Permitted hours and extensions

Chapter 14 - Betting and gaming

Chapter 16 - Gaming machines

Chapter 16 - Entertainment and copyright

Chapter 17 - Children and young persons

Chapter 18 - Visitors, guests and the public

Chapter 19 - Stewards and other staff

Chapter 20 - Dissolution and winding-up

need the approval of the Financial Services Authority (FSA) for the change of rule which will change your name. After that, you must hold a general meeting of the club. This decision cannot be taken by the committee alone.

You will then have to notify the relevant authorities, as mentioned in your rules, including the clerk to the magistrates, who keeps a record of your registration under the Licensing Act.

Unfortunately, a change in rules for a registered industrial and provident society requires the payment of a large fee. It might be advisable to look at your rules carefully and see if any other changes are required at this time, so that you could make all the necessary amendments at the same time, and so save some money.

7 What is Schedule 7?

Q I have heard a great deal about Schedule 7 of the Licensing Act 1964 with regard to the constitution of a members' club and should like to know whether it is absolutely binding on all clubs and that they must comply with all sections in order to become registered?

A That is the general impression given in many quarters. However, it is not strictly accurate in law. Schedule 7 covers club rules, especially the procedure for management of the club by an elective committee, general meetings, excluding people from voting and election of members. What is meant by an 'elective committee' is also spelled out in detail in the Schedule.

The magistrates have regard to the Schedule in deciding whether the club qualifies for registration under section 41 of the Licensing Act. Under that section, the main qualifications for registration are:
- The club is established and conducted in good faith as a club and has not less than 25 members.
- The supply of liquor on the premises is made by or on behalf of the club .
- The control of liquor is in the hands of a properly elected committee.
- No-one receives a commission or percentage on liquor purchases by the club
- No-one derives a profit from the supply of liquor to members.
- There must be a two-day wait for membership to take effect.

If the club rules do comply with schedule 7, then the court will assume that the club complies with the first three points outlined above. But they are empowered to look very carefully at the direction of club funds, any restrictive 'tie' on purchases and at the way the club's account books are kept.

It may be that certain clubs which are operated entirely bona fide do not have rules which comply exactly with schedule 7. This may not, all things being considered, preclude them from registration, as long as the magistrates are satisfied on the main qualifications above.

The purpose of the part of the Licensing Act dealing with registration in general is to ensure that, as far as is possible, the management of the club is in the hands of its members and in particular that the supply of liquor is managed by persons elected from among the membership and that the proceeds of the supply of that liquor go to the benefit of the members as a whole.

While there may be a proprietorial element in a number of registered clubs (such as employee sports clubs provided by companies), this will not in itself preclude registration if the day-to-day management of the bar and liquor stock, the election of members and the holding of meetings is in the hands of the members.

8 How to affiliate

Q There has been a suggestion in this area that all the Catholic clubs should affiliate. Can you tell me what the definition is of an affiliated member and could they play the gaming machines and take part in 'members only' bingo sessions?

A Affiliation has been successfully used by a number of club organisations to allow visiting members of other clubs to enjoy a special status within the host club, but it must be approached with a great deal of care to ensure that all those involved know how to operate the scheme.

The magistrates have the power of veto over certain rules admitting non-members, but they cannot veto a rule made by any club to allow sales to members of another club if, among other things:

1. Both clubs exist for learned, educational or political objects of a similar nature; or,

2. Both clubs are workingmen's s clubs registered under the Friendly Societies or Industrial and Provident Societies Acts.

It would seem to me to be appropriate to devise an affiliation scheme based on (1) above, so that members of other Catholic clubs could be admitted immediately on production of an affiliation card or membership card and could make purchases from the host club bar.

If such persons were only admitted as guests, they would have to be bona fide guests of members and could not make purchases at the bar.

It would require the amendment of the rules of each of the participating clubs, with similar wording so that all clubs would achieve the same status. The wording should be such as to make it clear to the court that the concession was being sought under section 49(4)(h) of the Licensing Act 1964 and was to operate among Catholic clubs and for no other purpose.

A limited affiliation of this kind is far more likely to succeed than a wider change of rule which would in effect, open the club to many types of non-member.

9 What kind of club?

Q I have recently taken over a static caravan site with a club. How do I stand with regard to the licence for the bar, which I do not fully understand? And what about other sites in the locality who want to use our club facilities. Can we open the bar to them as well?

A Thank you for sending me a copy of your licence. It is not uncommon for a Part I justices' on-licence to be granted in these circumstances, which is made subject to club conditions. You are effectively a proprietary club, and condition 1(a) allows you to sell liquor to members of that club who are admitted under the rules.

There is likely to be a requirement under the rules that there should be a two-day wait between proposal for membership and admission to the club. However, once admitted, the members may use the club as often as you allow. There is nothing to prevent you accepting membership from other sites. But you cannot just allow members of the public to walk into the bar, even if they sign a book on the way in. That will result in prosecution.

My advice is for you to set up a proper membership scheme, involve the other

2 Reassuring the trustees

Q This is a long-established club and we are in the process of filling three vacancies for the office of trustee caused by death and resignation. I wish to be able to assure the candidates that they are fully indemnified financially in the event of the club being wound up with outstanding debts. Is there some legal way in which this can be ensured before they take office?

A Fortunately you have enclosed a copy of your rules, from which I see clear guidance on the question of the appointment and role of trustees in the club.

First of all, the rules state that there shall be three trustees, who shall be officers of the club (but not serve on the committee). They are to be elected at an annual or special general meeting of members and remain in office until death, resignation or removal by a resolution passed at a general meeting.

Later in the same rule, it states that the property of the club shall be vested in the trustees 'to deal with as directed by resolutions of the committee.' This is known as a bare trust and is quite correct for a members' club such as yours. It shows that the trustees are merely representing the interests of the club members as expressed by the elective committee and not operating independently.

This part of the rule concludes with the sentence: 'They shall be indemnified against risk and expense out of the club property.' This essentially means that they are entitled to claim any expenses, debts or fines resulting from carrying out their duties from the funds of the members.

This is as far as any indemnity for trustees can go. It follows that in the normal course of events no liability attaches to trustees because they can make a call for funds from the club accounts. They are not in a position to pledge the credit of members (and neither is the committee, unless the rules so provide), so that they will have to rely on funds being available to meet any claims against them personally.

In fact, unless a trustee has entered into some form of personal pledge (such as signing a charge upon his or her own property in respect of the club) it is unlikely that a personal claim for debts owed would result if the club was wound up. Where the debts occurred through the mismanagement or default of the committee, then the trustees could not be held personally liable, as their only function is to hold property on behalf of that committee. It follows that trustees should do all in their power to ensure that they are properly indemnified by the rules, as outlined in Question 1. Otherwise, the club must consider some form of incorporation which makes trustees unnecessary and which limits the liability of those involved under the law.

3 The need for deeds

Q Several years ago this club purchased a house for the steward and the deeds were signed by the three club trustees who were in office at the time. Since then, two of these have died and the other man, in his sixties, is no longer a trustee. Our trustees are elected annually for a period of three years, one position becoming vacant each year. What is your advice on the updating of the signatories on this deed?

A I think you must act as soon as you can to rectify this situation, which has clearly got out of hand. I am very surprised that the matter of trustees is treated in this way in your club.

First of all, trustees personally hold the title to all property owned by the club. The trustees didn't just sign a deed, all those years ago: they became the owners of the steward's house. At the moment, the house is owned solely by the surviving trustee and not, in fact, by the club.

All property owned by the club must be transferred to the trustees currently holding office. On the death, resignation or removal of any trustee. the club must make a legal transfer of the property concerned to the incoming person.

The outgoing trustee or, if he is dead, his personal representative, must sign a transfer to the new person of his interest. In your system of appointing trustees on a rotating election, there must be such a transfer every year, unless persons are available for re-election.

What seems more suitable is for a rule change to be effected, so that the change of trustee can be achieved in accordance with a club rule which will satisfy the Trustee Act and allow the chairman of the club, or other senior officer, to appoint new trustees and thereby vest the property in them without formal transfer.

The chairman can do this by executing a deed of appointment which, under the terms of the Trustee Act, will also vest the property.

I appreciate this sounds complicated, but you are dealing here with ownership of property, and once the initial formalities are completed you will have a far more satisfactory state of affairs than exists at present.

Clubs with a number of trustees and a system of appointment or selection by the committee are in a better position. Clubs still registered under the Friendly Societies Act, of course, have an in-built system to cope with such transfers.

4 The duty of trustees

Q An extremely difficult problem has arisen in our club, whereby one of the trustees is refusing to sign a document of sale that has received the approval of the committee and a general meeting of members. He maintains that he is the legal owner and cannot be forced to sign, as he disapproves of the sale (he was one of the founder members). What is the legal position?

A I appreciate that this places the club in a difficult position. You do not enclose details of the method of appointing trustees but in normal circumstances they will receive their authority to act for the club either by a deed of trust or by a resolution of a general meeting.

Under your own rules and many others they hold the property of the club on trust for the benefit of the members absolutely and in practice they are bound to carry out the instructions of the committee. They are not actually empowered to refuse a valid instruction given to them.

A different situation would arise if the committee attempted to force them to do something illegal. But in this case it appears to me that all they are required to do is to sell certain property on behalf of the club for a price which is acceptable both to the committee and to the members as a whole. I can see no valid legal reason for this trustee refusing to do his duty.

You have provision under your rules for an emergency general meeting to be called at short notice. If the sale is dependent upon this signature and the person concerned appears immovable then there are valid grounds for a resolution to remove him from office and appoint another trustee in his stead. This is a course which you must now contemplate.

If the power of appointment or removal of trustees is vested in the committee, the change can be effected even faster. But a change of trustee should only he made in these special circumstances and not on the whim of the committee over some relatively trivial issue.

5 Can secretary hold other post?

Q **Is there anything in our rules, or in civil or common law, that debars a member from holding the joint positions of secretary and trustee, or trustee and any other position, e.g. a member of the committee, officer or steward?**

A I note from your letter that yours is a political social club, but does not have registration either under the Friendly Societies Acts or Industrial and Provident Societies Acts.

These two Acts are important. Under existing friendly society law, the same person cannot be a trustee and either the secretary or the treasurer of a club. It may well be that, as many other clubs of your type are indeed registered under this Act, it was assumed that the rule applied equally to you. But it does not appear to do so.

That being said, it is often thought advisable that persons who are current officers of the club (as opposed to past officers) should not also be trustees. We return to the age-old problem of 'wearing two hats'. In law, the trustees are the servants of the club committee, appointed expressly to do what the committee tells them, as long as it is not illegal or contrary to the terms of the trust itself. This means that officers will be telling themselves what to do, which in some cases can create problems.

But there is nothing in law to prevent members of the committee from being trustees also, if the general body of club members (or the committee, according to some rules) thinks they would do the job well. The only joint role which might be seen as incompatible is that of trustee and steward because, as I have often stated, it is very difficult when a person is both employee and employer at the same time.

Clubs which are registered under the Industrial and Provident Societies Acts become incorporated associations and as such do not require trustees at all, because the property of the club is held in their corporate name.

6 Problem of debt

Q **Due to some mishandling by our former secretary, the club has run into debt. At our last committee meeting, two of the trustees said that they would authorise payment of one of the major debts which the committee wanted to delay. There was a heated debate on the issue. Do the trustees have power over finances in this way?**

A The extent of the authority of trustees depends very much on the nature of their appointment and the responsibilities which they have been given. But in general terms, I should say that they do not have power to over-ride a decision of the committee.

This being said, the circumstances of your own case are special. If the financial situation is very grave indeed, and there is any possibility of the club being insolvent, the trustees would wish to protect their own position as the named holders of the real property and the people who could be sued on behalf of the club.

While they are normally charged under the rules with acting on the instructions of the committee, they might claim an over-riding duty if the actions of the committee were either illegal, beyond its powers or would lead the club into a situation where it was continuing to operate while insolvent.

They cannot, of course, authorise any payment in their own right, unless they are signatories to the cheques of the club. It is not usual for this to be the case, but where they are signatories they can only be prevented from authorising these payments by an express instruction from the committee, as long as that was considered to be in the best interests of the club as a whole.

The committee, however, should not seek to place the club's own trustees in a position where they were likely to be made personally liable for debts incurred by the club.

7 Change of trustees

Q We are very dissatisfied with one of the trustees who causes a great deal of friction and disharmony within the club and at meetings. He uses his position to block many new ideas, and is often the only 'no' vote at committee meetings. Our rules state that consent of all trustees is required for certain financial expenditure. Is there any way we can remove this person? I enclose a copy of our rules.

A I note that in this respect your rule accords with the specimen rules in Appendix B. in that a majority of two thirds of the members present and entitled to vote at a general meeting is required for the removal of a trustee from office. A special resolution must be drawn up, together with another resolution which will result in the vesting of the club property in whoever is selected as a replacement. Depending on the circumstances of the club, this may be effected by deed, or it may require the signature of the outgoing member.

In practical terms, it would be better if the trustee concerned could be persuaded to resign, perhaps by someone who knows him well, for the benefit of the smooth running of the club. Removal from office should only be contemplated as a last resort in such circumstances. When he realises how serious the situation is, perhaps he will agree to stand down.

8 Trustee employed

Q Can you tell us whether it is illegal to have a trustee as a paid employee of the club? I refer to standing in for the steward on his day off, or on annual holiday. Does the same apply to committee members?

A I appreciate that certain members' clubs find it necessary to use volunteer staff during the year. It also seems fair that these persons receive payment for what they do, making them employees for the duration of their work.

However, it is not advisable to have any club official as an employee of the club during his term of office. There are good reasons why this is both undesirable and impracticable in club law.

Unlike a business there is no single employer in a club. The function of

Chapter 4
Club rules

1 Rules as contract

Q Can you explain what rules legally represent within a club and would it be possible to take court action to enforce club rules which were being disregarded?

A Put very simply, the rules of a club represent the contract terms which exist between the members, or the members and the proprietor. They bind every member who joins the club, whether or not he has expressly signed a form saying that he agrees to be so bound.

Joining a club creates the contract, and each member subsequently is bound by the same set of rules which apply to everyone else. He knows that if he breaks the rules in a particular way, the contract may be ended and he may be expelled.

It is not necessary that everyone should be seen to read the rules before joining the club. As with many other contract terms, the law presumes knowledge of the terms by the assenting party, whose responsibility it is to ensure that he knows just what he is involving himself with.

However, the rules must be made available to members and the conduct of the club must not conflict with what those rules state, particularly in the matter of members' rights and privileges. For example, a proprietor cannot arbitrarily withdraw certain privileges of membership which he has contracted to give, and legal action would lie if he tried to do this without notice and without redress.

In the case of a members' club, however, the courts would not be disposed to intervene in a matter of rules which was entirely one of internal management, although they might do so where some specific loss — either of rights, property or money — might be claimed. Thus, they have been particularly active in the matter of wrongful expulsion of members, or wrongful refusal to afford rights available to other members of the club.

2 Essential rules

Q We are in the process of re-drafting our club rules which are quite old. We should be grateful for your guidance on what are the essential aspects which the magistrates would be looking for in a registered club such as ours.

A In deciding whether a club is established and conducted in good faith as a members' club, the magistrates will look carefully at the rules, mainly to ensure that the control of the club, insofar as it can be, is in the hands of the members through an elected body.

They will see whether in their view the rules conform on certain essential matters with schedule 7 of the Licensing Act 1964, and if they do not, whether the discrepancies ought to be corrected or will not destroy the essential elements of good faith.

This means they are entitled to be flexible on certain issues concerning the management of the club, but will be firmer on other issues such as elections and committee constitution, which should be included in the rules.

● The first point is that the management of the club must be in the hands of an 'elective committee' or several committees with one having control of the general management of the club's affairs.

● Such a committee is defined in the schedule as one on which members serve for between one and five years, and for which annual elections are held with members retiring in some stated form of rotation (*for further details, see Chapter 7*).

● Then there must, under the rules, be a general meeting at least once in every year, and 15 months must not be allowed to elapse without such a meeting being held. Both the club committee and a stated number of members must be capable of summoning a general meeting at any time on reasonable notice.

● Voting at general meetings must be confined to members, and the principle of one person, one vote, must obtain. However, the rules may exclude certain classes from voting on all or specific issues (*see Chapter 9*).

● Members must be elected to the club either at a general meeting or by a committee of members. The rules must make provision for the name and address of such a person to be prominently displayed on the club premises for not less than two days before the election.

● If there are other classes of members admitted not in this way but by some other device (e.g. temporary membership) these must not be 'significant' in proportion to the total membership.

These are the principal aspects of the rules covered by schedule 7, but the magistrates may also make other suggestions concerning the rules in order to clarify such matters as they think are in the interests of ensuring adequate control and representation. However, they are only in a position to veto such rules as may conflict with the law, or over which they have some form of control, such as the admission of non-members under section 49 (*see Chapter 18*).

In Appendix B of this book you will find the framework of a set of rules which I consider cover most of the essential areas for a registered members' club.

3 Reprint of rules

Q We are shortly to reprint our rule book, and I would like to know whether it is in order to condense the amendments and extra rules, or whether we have to leave them all as they stand?

A I think it is an excellent idea to reprint your rule book. Judging by its present state, this should have been done years ago. You seem to have added an extra rule every time you made an amendment. You have even amended the amendments and added another rule for this. I am surprised anyone

Chapter 6
Officers and their duties

1 Roles reversed

Q For some time there has been an understanding in this club that the secretary and chairman make the decisions and the committee does what they say. When this was raised, the chairman stated that as officers of the club they were in the highest position in the club, and that the committee should basically 'rubber stamp' what was proposed to them. Is this the true position of such officers?

A Of course it isn't, and you probably know that yourself, or you would not have raised the issue in this way. What often happens is that the roles are reversed where a strong chairman or secretary takes control of a less-forceful committee within the club.

In truth, the secretary's role is one of providing a number of specialised services to the club and the committee, as outlined elsewhere in this chapter. Because of his intimate contact with the day-to-day running of the club, he probably knows more about the place than most of the committee. But in terms of decision-making, he must accept what the committee 'instructs' him to do.

As far as the chairman is concerned, his main function at meetings of the club or the committee is to ensure that the business of the day is conducted in an orderly and proper manner, and that the rules of the club are followed in matters of procedure. In that sense he has a certain authority over the committee, but it is only in this context, and not in the context of the decisions themselves. These can only be made by the elected committee as a whole, of which the chairman and the secretary may well be members.

The only way to reverse the current situation in your club is for the committee to assert itself more and refuse to accept dictatorial methods of running the club. The law may be on your side, but I don't really think that is the issue here.

2 President rules the roost

Q Our president says that he can call committee meetings at any time in his own right, and also that he can designate a member of the committee to take the chair in his absence. As secretary, I say he is wrong on both counts. Could you adjudicate on this matter?

A Your president has to abide by your rule book like any other member. He cannot make up his own rules as he goes along, however much he might like to from time to time!

Fortunately, the club rules which you have supplied cover both points. Meetings of the committee are to be held regularly on a fortnightly basis to conduct the affairs of the club. It should be necessary to call additional meetings only in a crisis, and the correct procedure is for the secretary to be requested to convene it. As I have written elsewhere, a casual meeting between individual members of a committee is not a proper committee meeting: *every* member is entitled to receive notice from the secretary.

On your second point, the rules are just as specific. In the absence of the president, either the vice-president *or an elected chairman* shall take the chair. This means that the committee elects from its own number a chairman for the meeting in question. A choice cannot be imposed by the absent president.

3 Delegating responsibility

Q One of the members of our committee keeps talking about 'delegating responsibility' in club matters. I have some idea what it means, but I am not entirely sure and would like you to explain it in simple terms.

A Delegation of responsibility assumes an importance in law when one is studying such things as responsibility for negligence or unlawful acts. In law, people do not just do things for themselves; they can often do things through the medium of another person, who acts as their servant or agent.

In general, if a servant acts outside his or her express instructions, or does something he or she was not authorised to do at all, then the employer will not be held responsible for the action.

But where responsibility has been delegated, it is as if the second person had been put in the place of the first, so that the proprietor of a club can put a manager in and delegate his responsibility for the running of the premises to him. That will not assist the proprietor in avoiding prosecution himself for any illegal sales or infringements by the manager in the course of the job he had been delegated to carry out on behalf of his employer.

This may seem like splitting hairs, but it has come into the reckoning also with a club barmaid. In one case, a committee member of an Industrial and Provident Society club was held *not* to be liable when one of the club barmaids sold liquor to non-members. The reasoning in that case was that there was no relationship of 'master and servant' between the committeeman and the barmaid which would make him responsible directly for her actions.

However, I do not think that case should be taken as permission for committees or club officers to turn a 'blind eye' to such offences by staff in the future, because there may be evidence either of knowledge or of ignoring or even condoning offences, which might well tip the decision the other way. Certainly this is the case even with registered clubs such as yours.

4 Chairman's role

Q Can you give me some guidance on the proper role of the chairman of a members' club? Our rules are silent on the actual functions and although I am fairly young I have been strongly supported by members

It would be unacceptable that five members of a committee, who might be a vociferous minority with their own point of view, could bind all the other members, and the club, by holding unannounced meetings of this kind.

12 'Ad hoc' committee

Q Would you please explain what the strict definition of the 'ad hoc committee' is, in relation to our club. Does it just mean informal, so that members get together when the opportunity arises, or is there another meaning?

A The answer to this question really leads on from the earlier one about a gathering of five committee members. This Latin phrase should not be taken to mean 'informal' or 'spontaneous.' The real meaning is *for this purpose* and it applies to circumstances where a committee or meeting is formed for a specific function or decision.

Thus, where it says in your rules that any alteration can only be made at a general meeting 'called for this purpose', that could truly be described as an *ad hoc* meeting of the club. There is nothing informal or spontaneous about it, in terms of its ability or the seriousness of what it may proceed to do.

13 Steward in chair

Q I have been asked by the sports committee of this club if I would chair their meetings. I am currently the club steward. I agreed to this, but the management committee have now told me that I am not entitled to hold this position. Can you please advise me?

A I consider that the committee are probably right to suggest that you should be debarred from holding this position in the club. The fact that you are an employee of the club is incompatible with membership, as I have observed before. You do not enclose the club rules, but I would assume that this chairmanship ought properly to be held by a member and might even be an elected post within the club.

It may well be that you get on very well with the present committee and that no apparent harm would be done. But all officers of the club whether directly or indirectly concerned with the supply of liquor, ought to be bona fide members, unless there is a specific salaried function such as club manager or steward, which job is itself controlled and supervised by an elective committee.

Control of club activities by non-members creates a situation which is unacceptable for the constitution of a genuine members' club.

14 Vested interest

Q We have a potentially difficult problem on which we would like your advice. For some time the husband of our steward has been on the committee. What happens if we come to debate or discuss salary, working conditions etc.? We cannot speak openly and clearly he has an interest. What should we do?

A Some club rules make it absolutely clear that employees, or their immediate families, cannot be members of the club. I consider that to make such persons honorary or special members is even worse; it puts them in a segregated membership position which can only cause embarrassment to everyone.

The position of employee and member is incompatible, and clubs should make a strict rule not to allow it.

This being said, the position in your club exists and has to be dealt with. The correct procedure, where discussion or voting is taking place, is for anyone with a vested interest to declare it and leave the meeting It should be remembered that a committee, like any other representative body, should act in a proper manner and conduct its affairs honestly and fairly. It should also be above suspicion. As with the law, a suggestion of bias taints the decisions made.

You should, and must, be free to make such comments and criticisms of your employees as you think fit. You have a duty to the membership to ensure that they get the best service and the best deal, as any employer would seek. Someone related to the employee is clearly not in a position to pass judgement on these matters.

In such circumstances, a committee member does not have the right to remain, even if he insists. The matter of bias can be raised as a point of order and ruled upon by the chairman, if necessary. I should have hoped that the member in question would recognise the correctness of the move and volunteer to absent himself, rather than be forced to leave.

15 Allowing a debate

Q At our AGM the very tricky problem of remuneration for committee members came up, but the chairman would not allow a debate on this, saying that it was a matter for the committee itself to decide. We feel that we were gagged on this occasion. Can the chairman cancel a debate in this way?

A From the club rules which you enclose, it would appear that yours is a genuine workingmen's club, with a proper constitution which allows for general meetings and extraordinary general meetings, which may be demanded by the members.

You do not say whether the matter of the remuneration of club officials formed the subject of a motion, or was put on the agenda. It may be that if it arose merely in the course of discussion, or under 'any other business', the chairman properly curtailed discussion in those circumstances. No matter of such importance should be raised casually. It must be fully and properly discussed in open meeting.

This means that if the chairman did seek to reserve to the committee the right to fix their own members' remuneration from club funds, he was acting improperly. There is only a general rule in your rule book on this matter, and it certainly does not vest in the committee the right to take decisions on such financial matters without reference to the membership.

There is also the question of committee members voting on their own rewards. Whether or not they actually vote, they have a vested interest in the subject, and their presence at the meeting is bound to influence the other committee members. This is most definitely a subject for open discussion at a general meeting, and it is up to you and other members to call such a meeting under your rule 29, and to frame a motion which may be discussed at such a meeting, either approving or disapproving the principle of remuneration for club officials.

You should bear in mind that great care must be taken where matters of payment

A It is best not to let procedure at club meetings lapse in the mistaken impression that this will allow a 'free flow' of ideas. In many cases it leads to discord and unpleasantness, where there is no firm direction in the matter of speeches.

The general rule is that, apart from the proposer of the motion, each member is allowed to address the meeting once. The exceptions are for points of order, which should be addressed to the chairman on procedural matters, and questions, which may be addressed to the speaker to clarify what has been said.

But these questions should not be allowed to develop into speeches in their own right. The chairman has a duty to curtail such attempts and ask the member concerned to put his question immediately. If he does not, the chairman may cut him short.

There is a convention that if the chairman stands, any member should sit, and other members may well shout 'Chair, Chair' if a member persists when the chairman is standing to make a ruling.

5 Motions and amendments

Q Could you give us some guidance on the correct formula for putting motions and amendments to a meeting? At our last AGM we got into a terrible mess and lost sight of the original motion, which has created a great difficulty for the secretary and myself as chairman.

A It is not unusual that without a very firm control of this aspect of general meetings, you end up by not being able to see the wood for the trees! When everyone has had a say, the original idea may have become somewhat obscure.

The first thing to ensure is that the motion itself is clearly stated on the agenda. This is a responsibility of the secretary, who may be first approached with the proposal. He should try to ensure that the proposer puts as clear and concise a motion as possible. There is a tendency to try and put the arguments rather than the facts into a motion for debate.

Any amendment proposed to this motion must seek to qualify it in some way, rather than directly contradicting or disagreeing with it. That is properly done by voting against the motion.

Any matters which are outside the scope of the motion, or which directly conflict with it, properly form the basis of a separate motion which should be delivered to the secretary before the meeting.

This is vital in matters affecting club rules. No amendment should be allowed to a proposal to amend club rules except alterations in wording to clarify it or remove ambiguity. If the proposal itself is found to be unsatisfactory it will be defeated.

The procedure for amendment is as follows. At any time during the debate, an amendment to the original motion may be proposed. The chairman must then ask for a seconder to the amendment. If he or she is found, the proposer of the amendment then has one speech in support of it. He does not have a right to sum up after the subsequent discussion.

The amendment is then discussed and put to the vote. If it is lost, the motion stands and debate continues, or the original motion is put. If it is carried, the motion itself will then be put as amended, or further discussion will take place, and further amendments may be proposed and seconded.

The chairman has a vital role in this, to ensure that the correct procedure is followed at all times. His job is to ensure that the meeting proceeds in a clear progression, from one point to the other, whatever the 'temperature' of the debate, or the issues raised. This is why it is so important that the chairman remains impartial and in some senses 'above' the debate taking place.

Once the complete motion has been put to the meeting, and carried, no further amendments can possibly be made, and the chairman must stress this to the members if necessary. If there have been a number of amendments, the chairman should carefully read the final motion to ensure that everyone knows exactly what is being voted on.

6 Any other business

Q Am I correct in thinking that there is a restriction on the business that can be transacted under the heading 'Any Other Business' at a club Annual General Meeting? Our rules state that no business other than that specified in the agenda shall be transacted, except with the consent of the majority of members present.

A I am aware that this item poses a problem in many clubs. I have said before that this item is not a repository for everyone's pet subject and certainly is not a time when substantial proposals should be put to the meeting.

This is a time when the chairman should exercise firm control on the members and not allow an item to be debated which should have formed the basis of a motion to be placed on the agenda. The correct use of 'Any Other Business' is to convey to the widest audience of members any specific points, announcements or forthcoming events. It is also an opportunity for individual members to put questions or observations to officers.

But if a member seeks to put a specific proposal under this heading, he should be immediately informed by the chairman that the matter cannot be decided on at the time and should be communicated in writing to the secretary for possible inclusion at the next meeting.

As you are aware, any proposals which do arise spontaneously at the AGM, cannot be used to change the rules or bind the committee in any way. The committee is entitled to treat such discussion as for information only, and is not obliged to act on it.

7 Method of voting

Q Is it obligatory in a registered members' club for voting to be by ballot on specific motions, or on elections of officers, or can voting take place in a manner decided by the club?

A There is no requirement, unless it is stated in the rules, that voting should be by any specific method, as long as it is seen to be fair and just. Some clubs make it a rule that the conduct of elections should be by ballot, rather than just a show of hands. But when voting on motions, or on changes in the rules, a show of hands at the meeting is a clear enough indication of the intentions of members.

Where there is a large meeting, tellers should be appointed to ensure that the counting of votes for and against proceeds in an orderly fashion. Where there is any doubt on the show of hands, the chairman should call for a count and may himself appoint tellers if none has been selected for the job.

I have often commented that I consider it inappropriate in the case of an equality of votes in a general meeting of members that the chairman should exercise a casting vote. Apart from the accepted constitutional position that each member has one vote only, to decide an issue on a second vote from the chair in a large meeting is inappropriate for major issues. If a motion cannot secure a proper majority it should be lost.

8 Vote contrary to rule-book

Q At a recent AGM of the club a motion was recorded as carried, but when writing up the minutes I realised that this was not in accordance with the rules, the requisite majority not having been achieved. Neither the chairman nor the president realised this had happened. My question is: what happens about the motion? Is it valid as passed or must it be declared void and voted on again?

A You do not indicate what motion was actually put to the meeting, but I assume it was one which required, for example, a two thirds majority of those present and voting or entitled to vote, and that the required majority was not obtained.

This indicates that it was either a rule change or a financial change of some importance. The matter cannot therefore be allowed to rest and the mistake 'forgotten', now that it has been realised. If you do this, then a member could challenge the right to make the change at some time in the future. This is particularly important if it involved, for example, a change in subscription rates or qualifications for membership.

There are two courses open to you. You will have to call an extraordinary general meeting to vote again on the issue, or you will have to post a notice declaring the vote invalid, and saying that the matter will have to be raised again at next year's AGM.

If action has already been taken on the basis of a valid motion, then the former course seems acceptable, with a provision that it should have retrospective effect from the date of the AGM. But what surprises me about this question is that those who opposed the motion (and there must have been a number who did) did not themselves spot the error at the time.

There is usually an eagle-eyed member who knows the rule-book backwards and is quick to point out procedural irregularities. Certainly, you as secretary must bear some responsibility with the chairman for not being fully conversant with the rules on the question of voting. Some clubs place on the agenda the voting requirements where they are stipulated in the rules.

Make sure in future that you have checked on all aspects of voting procedure and qualification immediately prior to the Annual General Meeting, so that members' questions or points of order can be answered quickly and succinctly.

9 Called for the purpose

Q We seek your help on the meaning of one of our rules concerning certain meetings of the club. In two cases it states that matters may only be discussed and voted on 'at a meeting called for the purpose'. Does this have to be a separate meeting, or can we incorporate it in, for example, our AGM?

A The object of including this phrase is to ensure that members are made aware of the subject matter of the meeting which they are summoned to attend. It sometimes happens that the wording of the notice summoning the meeting is too vague, and this can lead to confusion.

There is, however, nothing to prevent a meeting being called for more than one purpose. For example, your rule on the amendment of the rules themselves states that they may only be changed 'at a meeting called for the purpose', but the AGM is an obvious platform for this, and the rule change can be included in the purposes of the meeting.

It is a common problem among clubs that the notice convening a special general meeting is often defective in its statement of purpose. The best practice is to ensure that only the specific subject is mentioned, and there must be an avoidance of any item such as 'any other business' at such a meeting. Nor can members introduce other items for discussion. The chairman of the meeting must instantly halt any attempt to broaden the discussion or introduce new topics.

An example is the difference between 'a resolution to change the rules on family membership' and 'a proposal that rule 15(c) be amended as follows...' The former allows wide-ranging discussion on the members' attitudes to family membership; the latter contains a specific proposal for a rule change on the same subject which, if passed by the required majority, will operate to change the club rules there and then.

If members start to discuss associate membership or visitors during this meeting, the chairman is entitled to bring the debate back to the specific subject in question.

10 Rule change illegal

Q The general secretary and assistant secretary resigned in March, having been elected at the AGM. The committee then nominated a co-opted member as secretary and a section representative as assistant.

Under pressure they then called a special general meeting at which only 29 members were present. The new secretary conducted the business, which was his own election, and also introduced a set of revised rules. Under our old rules, 75 members form a quorum at a general meeting. What should be done?

A It appears from the two sets of rules which you have enclosed that the actions which you describe are unconstitutional and could be set aside if the members so decided. Although it would appear that the committee does have power to co-opt other members to fill vacancies, the resignation of officers is a more serious matter and should be dealt with at a special meeting of the club.

Such a meeting must be convened in accordance with the rules and should deal with a specific matter, such as the election of new officers. You do not make it clear how this rule revision came about, but the changes made are very important and deserve a separate meeting for discussion. It seems odd that rule revisions of this nature were not dealt with at your AGM this year.

The most important point is that the meeting was inquorate under your existing rules, which require 75 members to be present before business can be conducted. An inquorate meeting can, of course, continue, but it is informal and cannot make decisions on behalf of the club. It certainly would be most improper to conduct elections at such a meeting, and the changes in rules adopted there are invalid. Your existing rules, therefore, still apply.

Your committee must attempt to gain a quorum at another properly convened general meeting if it wishes to proceed with rule changes. If they refuse to do so, you will have to call a special general meeting yourself to raise the issue. The last resort is to the courts, to compel the committee to act in accordance with the rules. On such a step you would have to consult a solicitor, who would advise you on the procedure.

11 Change of supplier

Q Recently the management committee of this club orally agreed to accept the offer of another brewery to supply the club with intoxicating liquor. They had offered good financial benefits and the correspondence was nearly complete. The members then requested an extraordinary general meeting with a proposal that we do not change from our present supplier and the resolution was passed on a majority vote. Our rule 32 states that the supply of liquor shall be under the sole control of the management committee. Is this overturned by the resolution and do we need to inform the registration authorities?

A Under the conditions for the grant of a club registration certificate, the rules must provide for the right of ordinary members to call an extraordinary general meeting of the club, if a specified number of them join together to do so.

Your rules provide for ten members to requisition such a meeting, at which a specific subject should be entered for discussion and, if required, a resolution passed by the members on that subject.

However, at the time of the meeting, the club was governed by its existing rules, a copy of which you have sent me. This makes it clear that the management committee are solely responsible for the purchase and supply of intoxicating liquor for the club.

While it is perfectly possible for an extraordinary general meeting to make recommendations to the club committee, it is not possible for a resolution passed in this way to bind that committee's actions. The committee should, of course, take note of the resolution, but any change in policy will be theirs to decide.

This being said, if the committee are charged with running the club 'for the benefit of the members' then they should pay attention to the wishes of members concerning the beer they drink. It is surprising that this matter should have come so far, and that the committee is so out of touch with the tastes of its membership. If the financial deal is in the best interests of the club as a whole, this should have been explained to the dissenters.

There has been no change of rules and no notification needs to be made to the clerk to the magistrates under section 48 of the Licensing Act 1964.

12 Requisition rule

Q We are a registered sports club and have just submitted some rule changes to our local police inspector. He has said that our rule on special general meetings is wrong concerning the number of people to sign a request. It should read 'not more than 30'. What is your opinion?

A What you are doing submitting your rules to the police is anyone's guess. However, such a suggested rule is quite wrong and is contrary to schedule 7 to the Licensing Act 1964. It must be far more specific than this.

The schedule states that the club members themselves 'must be capable of summoning (a general meeting), or requiring one to be summoned (by the secretary) at any time on reasonable notice if a specified number of them join to do so.'

The schedule then goes on to say that this number must not be more than 30 nor more than one-fifth of the total membership.

As you can see, the phrase 'not more than 30' is not a specified number at all. It could, in fact, be two, or twenty, or twenty-nine. The club rules **must** give the number of signatories required on the requisition **as a number**.

If the total of ordinary members of the club is less than 150, the specified number must indeed be less than 30. For example, where the club membership hovers around 100, only 20 members would be needed to call such a meeting. The wording of the rule should be 'provided that he receives a request signed by at least 20 members of the club that such a meeting should be held and giving the specific reason for the meeting'.

Clubs which are registered under the Friendly Societies or Industrial and Provident Societies Acts are not required to comply with every aspect of schedule 7, and it may be that they sometimes exceed the limitations set down here. But most of the rules which I have seen stay within the recommendations of schedule 7.

13 Requisition not quorum

Q Our club rules state that a special general meeting can be called by 30 members or by the general committee. The committee called such a meeting at which only 23 members of the club were in attendance. One member claimed that the meeting could not continue as the required 30 members were not present. As chairman I ruled that this interpretation was not correct, as this was only for signatures to call such a meeting. Can you give us your ruling on this?

A Under rule 9, a special general meeting may indeed be called if a specified number of members join together to do so. It also correctly states that the committee itself can call a special meeting, which I assume was what happened in this case. The question seems to be: what should the quorum be to make such a meeting valid under the rules?

Unfortunately, your rules say nothing on this point and no minimum number of members is given to validate such a meeting. This can be stated in the byelaws of the club and your rules do in fact provide for byelaws to be made. It is an important matter, as the current situation shows, and steps should immediately be taken to add a minimum number for a quorum both for general and committee meetings.

As things stand, any number of members may gather together and elect a chairman and conduct a valid meeting. The fact that a special general meeting may be called by a requisition signed by thirty members does not mean that the quorum for that meeting is automatically set at the same number.

As this meeting was called at the request of the committee, if the required notice had been given to members then the meeting was totally in order and able to deal with the subject under discussion. A resolution passed by such a meeting would also be valid, unless it sought to change the rules, as this may only be done, in your club's case, at an annual general meeting.

14 Chairman's rights

Q We seek your advice on a matter of procedure at meetings. Is it true that if the chairman of a general meeting of the club stands up, the member currently speaking must sit down, or must the member be allowed to continue with his speech?

A Your long letter makes it clear that this is part of a wider problem in the club at present, concerning a major difference of opinion. However, your question raises an important point which should be of interest to many members' clubs.

Adherence to procedure at meetings has one object — to ensure that the meeting runs smoothly and that what happens is clear to those attending. If a meeting descends into argument or uncontrolled discussion, that clarity is lost, confusion exists and important matters are not resolved.

It may seem pointless and time-consuming to go through some of the rituals, but they are designed to regulate what happens and they act as an important safety valve.

Unless the rules of the club provide for the club chairman or some other officer to take the chair at such meetings. a chairman has to be elected at the start of the meeting. After his election, the chairman has full power to control the meeting, and if it lapses into disorder he may declare the meeting adjourned and leave the chair. If he does so, any attempt to continue the meeting with another chairman will be invalid.

The chairman also take precedence over all other speakers and no speaker should remain standing if the chairman rises, or rise to speak while he is speaking. His duty is to maintain order and ensure each member receives a fair hearing. He should act impartially but he must exercise control, including the prevention of a member from continuing a long speech beyond his allotted time, or speaking for a second time when others have not spoken.

15 Notice of meetings

Q Can you tell me the minimum period of notice required for calling a meeting of club members, and also whether there is any difference between the AGM and other meetings called at the request of members? One such meeting was recently called at four days' notice to discuss a matter of great importance, and many members were not present.

A I am amazed to note that there is no period of notice for the calling of meetings laid down in your rules. This is a bad omission and your club should take immediate steps to pass a byelaw giving minimum periods of notice.

In general, the rules should state when the annual general meeting is to be held. This need not be a specific day, but it is best if the month can be given (e.g. 'in the month of May in every year... ').

It is important to note that under the terms of the Licensing Act for registered clubs, l5 months must not elapse without a general meeting of members.

The rules must cover elections to the committee every year, so that there must be a time for nominations to be accepted, and a closing date for nominations. There must also be a time for motions to be received, so that these can be placed on the agenda.

So that the secretary can give proper notice of the subject of meetings, motions should be received by a date not later than 14 days before the meeting. Even this is a fairly short time, and three weeks would be better.

The date of the annual general meeting, where it is not fixed specifically by the rules, should also be notified to members well in advance, and a minimum period should be specified, ideally more than one month in advance of the date fixed. The earlier notification is given, the better it is.

As far as other general meetings are concerned, the period of notice may have to be shorter, but there should still be an adequate time given to enable as many members as possible to attend. You do not state the reason for which this recent meeting was called, but however important the matter, it would seem that the members' interests as a whole require a longer notice. After all, unless the committee agrees to be bound by the meeting's decision or unless a rule change or dissolution of the club is to be voted on. a motion, passed at such a meeting is merely a recommendation.

Rule changes or dissolution certainly require far longer notice than four days, and all periods of notice, if not contained in the club rules themselves, should be immediately framed into byelaws for adoption at the next committee meeting.

16 Visitors at AGM

Q On the evening of our AGM can the club be closed to everyone except members? One of our committee has suggested that for an AGM anyone is entitled to attend and listen to the proceedings.

A The annual general meeting of a members' club is a private occasion. It is the main opportunity for every member of the club to hear an up-to-date account of the club's affairs and to voice his opinions, if he wishes.

But this is essentially a private matter. The club is not obliged to present a report to anyone else, except in the case of clubs which have certain external obligations, such as those registered under the Friendly Societies or Industrial and Provident Societies Acts, or where a branch club has to file accounts with the head office of the Association.

It is certainly not true that members of the public have a right to attend this meeting. Indeed, they are normally specifically excluded from the premises, unless they are a genuine guest of a member or are allowed in on a special occasion as a visitor.

If a meeting is confined to members only, it makes certain procedural matters easier. For example, voting may be by a simple show of hands, rather than a complicated members-only count. Of course, voting at any club meeting, on any issue, must be confined to full members who are declared under the rules to have voting rights.

As far as the club premises are concerned, it may often be possible to close just the meeting itself to non-members, because it is likely that there will be members on the door to prevent, if necessary, unauthorised persons from entering that part of the club. It may be more practicable to restrict entry to the club to members only for that evening, posting a notice to that effect by the entrance for some time prior to the date, to give all club users advance warning.

17 Minutes required

Q I am in dispute with this club over the question of the last AGM minutes. I tried to bring this matter up at an extraordinary general meeting of the club called to discuss another matter, but was ruled out of order. What is the legal position?

A Unfortunately you do not enclose your rules. but I understand that your club is registered under the Friendly Societies Acts, so I can make certain assumptions about them. First of all, I think it was correct that you should be ruled out of order at the extraordinary meeting. Unless the matter under discussion directly concerned the minutes of the previous AGM, then no discussion over those minutes can be allowed.

The chairman of such a meeting has an obligation to restrict discussion only to the matter or matters raised in the notice to the meeting; it would be improper to allow extraneous items to be raised when members have had no prior notification.

On the question of the minutes themselves, all clubs should keep an accurate record of meetings in a book kept for the purpose, which should be open to inspection at any reasonable time by any member of the club. This is a requirement of the Friendly Societies Act, so that your club secretary is obliged to make the minutes of the last AGM available to you for inspection.

You must, of course, allow a reasonable time for the minutes to be written up, but they must constitute a true and accurate record of the principal happenings of the meeting. It is not a requirement that every word should be transcribed, but equally they must cover the order of events and votes, including figures where necessary.

If for any reason you consider that the minutes are inaccurate, you are entitled to raise the matter at the next AGM, when the previous minutes will be adopted by the meeting.

The only question to be decided is if the record is accurate. This is no time to raise specific items decided at that meeting, or to attempt to change resolutions taken at that time. The chairman must seek to determine the accuracy of the minutes and any other discussion must be curtailed until later in the meeting.

You are entitled to appeal to the Financial Services Authority if the club minutes are not made available to you, or if they are not presented to the subsequent AGM of the club for approval by the body of members.

18 Forgotten minutes

Q At our recent AGM there was some heated discussion and confusion at the beginning of the meeting, and after the chairman had closed the meeting it was discovered that the minutes of the previous AGM had not been read. Some members claimed the whole meeting was invalid and should be held again. Can you give us a ruling, please?

A An omission of this kind does not invalidate the whole meeting if it was properly convened in accordance with the rules and there were sufficient members present to form a quorum.

All the other matters which were dealt with at that meeting will therefore stand. The fact that the proper procedure was not followed should have been pointed out from the floor on a point of order. Strictly speaking, it is one of the secretary's functions to record the minutes of meetings and ensure that the correct procedure is followed.

It is always helpful to have an agenda for the meeting, and for the secretary to check each item as it arises.

The object of 'reading the minutes' is to ensure that they stand as a true and accurate record of what took place. It follows that only those persons who were present at the previous meeting can vote on their accuracy. Minutes must not be changed at the following meeting unless they are inaccurate in matters of fact. Any change in policy or decisions must be properly presented again as a motion and voted on by those present.

It would seem appropriate for the minutes to be published in some way — either on the club notice board or by circulation to members. If any member has a suggested correction, it may be necessary to call an extraordinary general meeting to approve a change in the record. Otherwise, it would seem sensible to let matters rest.

19 Chairman's vote

Q Under our rules it states that the chairman shall have a casting vote at all meetings of the club. What does this mean in practice?

A As you are a registered club, your rules should as far as possible comply with those in schedule 7 to the Licensing Act 1964. They are not absolutely binding, but the court may have regard to them in deciding whether the club is properly established and conducted.

Under that schedule, voting at any general meeting of the club must be confined to members, and all members 'must have equal voting rights'. A strict interpretation of that condition would mean that the chairman, as a club member, would be restricted to one vote, like everyone else.

Schedule 7 does not deal with voting at committee meetings, and it is generally accepted that where necessary the chairman may have a casting vote on issues where there has been an equality of voting. This means an extra vote in addition to the one he has already cast. It does not mean simply delaying his own vote.

My own view is that the best policy is only to pass resolutions or change the course of a club where there is a clear majority in favour of the action. If the chairman is faced with an equality of voting, it is obvious that a majority of persons present are not in favour of the proposal. Consequently, he should vote against the motion.

The reason for this is that it would be more unfair to use a casting vote to tip the balance for a new rule, or a change, than it would be to vote against so that the matter can be raised again. To rely on a casting vote to decide important issues can lead to friction within the club.

20 Proxy voting

Q At our recent AGM a person turned up who used to be a member but has not been to the club for some time, saying that he had come to vote 'proxy' for one of our key members. He was allowed to take part in the discussions, but after some debate he was not allowed to vote. Can you say whether we acted correctly? I enclose our club rules.

A Your club rules and byelaws say nothing at all about proxy voting. This type of representation is allowed for certain types of clubs, but even then special arrangements have to be made. Non-members cannot just 'turn up' at the door and expect to take the place of a full member of the club.

In my view the person concerned should not have been allowed to take part in any discussion if he was not a member, unless the body of the meeting had voted to allow him to address them.

Some clubs specifically exclude non-members from attending the AGM, on the grounds that the private affairs of the club should only be discussed by current members. There is nothing wrong in this practice.

Where the club has an active section of members with limited or no voting rights, it is sometimes felt that they should have a 'voice' at such meetings. This is good practice, but depends entirely on the internal management of the club.

Under the terms of the Industrial and Provident Societies and the Friendly Societies Acts, proxy voting is allowed in certain strictly controlled circumstances on special resolutions. The same system can be extended to ordinary resolutions, as long as the rules of the club allow. Otherwise, a person must be present in order to register a vote.

Under the rules for clubs contained in the Licensing Act, each club member is entitled to one vote, and voting at general meetings must be confined to members. A strict interpretation of that might mean that proxy voters who were not club members would not be allowed at all.

21 What majority?

Q **At our AGM there was a problem about a rule change, which under our rules requires a two-thirds majority. I enclose our rule book and would be grateful if you could clarify whether this means a majority of those voting 'yes' or 'no', a majority of those entitled to vote or a majority of those actually present, including abstainers.**

A Your rules are inadequate on this question, stating that rule changes may be passed 'by a two-thirds majority'. In most rule books this is expressed as 'two thirds of the members present' or 'two thirds of the members present and entitled to vote'. This seems to me to be the correct interpretation, particularly for rule changes.

If there is a fixed proportion required for the passing of a rule change, then it is absolutely **essential** that there is some way of checking how many voting members are actually present, particularly if you allow non-voting attendees at the meeting. This means that if 90 voting members are present at the meeting, at least 60 'yes' votes will be required for a rule change, however many vote against or abstain. For this system to be effective, there must be some check on the number of members present at the time of the vote, usually on admission. Alternatively, the tellers must count all votes and abstentions and work out the proportions on the spot.

22 Writing a resolution

Q **We wish to call an extraordinary general meeting of the club to discuss an issue of concern to a number of members. What would be the effect if our resolution is passed: does it bind the committee to take the action**

we request? I enclose a copy of what we have written.

A Great care should be taken in the framing of resolutions for such meetings. Only the matters contained in such a resolution are entitled to be discussed and the chairman of the meeting can rule out any discussion which goes beyond the proposal.

However, there is nothing in your rules which would prevent a proposal at an EGM to change the rules of the club, which would have the effect you desire. Such changes are not reserved entirely for the annual general meeting of the club but they do require at least a two-thirds majority of those present and entitled to vote. Your rules also state that notice of an EGM must be given to each member, so it is important that the resolution should be properly framed.

If the rule change is carried, then the committee must abide by it and cannot seek to veto it. In the circumstances, they may consider this to be a vote of no confidence, as the majority of them oppose such a change and therefore if the rule change is passed they may consider it appropriate to resign. In such circumstances your rules would allow for elections to be held as soon as possible to ensure a new committee to take over the affairs of the club.

In many clubs where the power to change the rules is confined to the AGM, an extraordinary general meeting of this kind could only make a recommendation to the committee, which they could either accept or reject

It should be remembered that they retain the overall control of the club for the period of their election.

23 Called to the bar

Q During our AGM there was a vote on a crucial issue and when the result was announced some members protested that people eligible to vote were in the bar at the time of the vote. They demanded a fresh vote with these persons present. This vote was different from the first one. What is the constitutional position? I enclose our club rules to assist you.

A I take it there was considerable pressure upon you at the time, but I do not think you should have allowed the second vote to be taken. In accordance with your rules, the time and place for the annual general meeting of the club is circulated to all members personally. A notice as to the time and place is also posted in the clubhouse, for all members to read.

There is therefore no excuse for persons who are members and eligible to vote not knowing when and where the meeting is to be held.

It is thereafter their responsibility to attend if the wish to join in the discussion and vote on the issues. Those persons who do not attend the club on that evening forfeit their right to vote and allow those present to deal with the business as it arises.

I take it that an agenda was agreed and made available to those present. If all these formalities have been complied with, then the voting may take place as and when the meeting decides.

Members who are not present at the time the vote is taken (unless there is provision for proxy or postal voting in the rules) are disenfranchised. They cannot subsequently claim a right which they failed to exercise at the correct time. There appears to be no obligation under your rules or byelaws for you to ring a 'division bell' or to announce the vote throughout the club.

One must ask why these missing members were in the bar at the time of the

QUESTIONS & ANSWERS ON CLUB LAW

vote? Even if they left the meeting in order to obtain refreshments, they could have intimated to someone that they wished to vote and ask to be summoned at the correct time. But the onus is on them to be present. Their absence does not invalidate the first vote.

My view is that the first vote stands and the second vote is void. If the matter is to be raised again, it must be made the subject of a fresh motion for another general meeting of the club.

24 Committee men can vote

Q Recently a motion of 'no confidence' was put down for the next meeting of our club, as the members feel that the committee has let them down. My question is: can the committee members themselves vote on this motion? Our feeling is that they cannot, as it directly involves them personally.

A The rules of your club clearly state that each ordinary member of the club may vote at any general meeting. Only ordinary members may stand for committee, therefore I assume that all members of the committee are ordinary members of the club. This means that the committee may vote as ordinary members on any issue raised at a general meeting, whether it affects them personally or not.

You cannot disenfranchise committee members on this issue. Of course they are going to vote against the motion, but that is not the point. They are entitled to express their views and if they feel that members have not got the full facts, or have come to an erroneous decision, then they must be allowed to say so, and to vote against you.

You must remember that this motion is merely a resolution. It is not legally binding on the committee, nor are they legally obliged to resign if the vote goes against them. But clearly they must consider their position if the majority of the members feel that they are not doing their job properly.

It is often interesting to look at Parliamentary procedure in these respects. The opposition from time to time may ask for a vote on a motion of no confidence in the government. Does that mean that government ministers must abstain on the issue? Of course not. They vote against the motion, because they think they are doing the right thing. If the vote goes against them, however, it is clear that they cannot continue in government (unlike a club committee) because they will be outvoted subsequently on important issues.

Committee members might decide to abstain on such an issue, because they want to see what support they have from the ordinary members. But they are not obliged to do so.

Chapter 10
Members' rights and obligations

1 Member sues club?

Q Can you tell me if there are any circumstances in which a member can sue his own club? I seem to remember reading some time ago that this was not possible, but has there been a change in the law?

A In chapter 1, I explained how an unincorporated members' club had no legal identity and therefore could not be sued in its own name. In addition to this problem, there is indeed a general principle that a member cannot sue his own club for damage, loss or injury, because he would effectively be suing himself!

As far as claims for damage or negligence are concerned, the other members of the club owe him no duty of care, so that, for example, if he slips on wet leaves or snow, or is injured on the club premises, he cannot claim for negligence against the club as occupier, because he is *also* the occupier.

His only recourse in such circumstances is to attempt to claim against the individual who caused him the damage, if he could be found. But where that person was acting in the course of his duties, such as the steward or groundsman, the matter might well come right back to the fact that it was the member, jointly with everyone else, who employed him!

This general principle was thought to be universal among members' clubs, but it has now been qualified by an important case decided in 1994. This held that where a club was incorporated in some way (the most common being registration under the Industrial and Provident Societies Act 1965), there would be a body separate from the individual member which could be held to owe them a duty of care. In that case, a lady member of a workingmen's club was found able to pursue a claim against the club as a 'visitor' under the Occupiers' Liability Act because the club had a separate identity from her. She had slipped on a slope when leaving the club and sustained injuries for which she attempted to sue. The High Court found that a club could owe a duty of care even to its own shareholders.

It seems that registration under the Friendly Societies Acts would not deliver the same result, because there is no actual incorporation and the trustees merely hold the property on behalf of the members as a whole. Such is the way of the law!

Incorporated clubs should therefore ensure that they have adequate insurance cover for claims both from members and visitors to the premises.

2 Damages for expulsion

Q Is there any way in which a member can realistically take legal action against his own club? I was thinking about cases of wrongful expulsion and the like, where people threaten to sue the club.

A It is true that where there is a cause of action which relates to the contract which has been made between the individual member and the other members, such as expulsion from membership, or removal of rights, then the courts may well eventually be involved.

Such action is rare and will depend to a great extent on the club rules and the methods laid down there for the resolving of disputes. Particular instances are quoted in this chapter.

The rules of Friendly Societies and Industrial and Provident Societies contain provision for arbitration in the case of disputes involving members or past members and the society, and even for persons claiming through members.

In serious cases the Financial Services Authority, which has taken over the role of Registrar, provides a system of arbitration which is very similar to certain court procedures.

There is one basic point on the law in this area. The courts will not intervene where the rules leave the matter to the discretion of the club committee and that body has acted within its powers. You cannot expect a form of 'justice' from the courts which will overturn a decision with which you disagree. By agreeing to abide by the rules, you also place yourself at the 'mercy' of the committee, and must usually accept their decision as final.

3 A member's liability

Q I know that most club members don't think much about the law when they join a club, but could you tell me whether the ordinary member takes on any financial obligation if, for example, the committee or officers run the club so badly that there are huge debts. Could someone come round to every member and demand they pay their share?

A Fortunately, there is a leading case on this very point in which the law on members' liability is stated very clearly. In general, a member only contracts to pay what he directly owes to the club, and no more. He does not take on, if you like, a form of corporate liability for actions over which he has no direct control.

At the beginning of this century, a learned judge commented: 'the feature which distinguishes (members' clubs) from other societies is that no member as such becomes liable to pay to the funds of the society or to anyone else any money beyond the subscriptions required by the rules of the club to be paid, so long as he remains a member. It is upon this fundamental condition, not usually expressed but understood by everyone, that clubs are formed'.

What this means is that the individual member cannot, as your question suggests, be held liable by some outside creditor for a proportion of the debt which he is owed by the club. The usual recourse of such persons is to the trustees or officers of the club, in the first instance, and subsequently to the persons ordering or calling for the goods or service. At no stage is he given the legal right to pursue individual members in respect of the debt.

4 Expelled from club or branch?

Q This club is also the headquarters of the local branch of the British Legion. Ten days before our AGM we expelled a member from the club in accordance with our rules, a copy of which I enclose. He then was present at the AGM, insisting that he was still a member of the branch and could attend when branch business was being discussed. After some argument he refused to leave, saying that he hadn't voted. I called the police and he was removed. What is the legal position?

A Your rules are clear on the matter of expulsion. If the committee have been through the correct procedure and decided to expel the member, then all the privileges of membership are removed from him, including his right to use the club facilities.

As far as voting is concerned, your rules once again state that a person may be disqualified by suspension or expulsion. This seems obvious, because termination of membership makes a person a member of the public with no rights on the club premises, except those allowed by the club committee.

Your relationship with the branch, however, does need clarification. You are entitled as a club to refuse admission to an expelled person for whatever purpose, and this person's membership of the branch does not over-ride your rights over the conduct of the club premises. However, if the branch and club rules differ, so that a person may remain a member of the former while expelled from the latter, then you must look to the branch rules for guidance on a member's rights. If there is a conflict (in that a branch member may be entitled to access to his branch premises for meetings), then you should seek to resolve it with the branch secretary.

Meanwhile, the person concerned may be banned from the club premises and you will be acting in accordance with your rules in enforcing the ban.

5 Members' produce

Q What if a member brings his own garden produce from his allotment and sells it to other members, is this not private gain? Should it be allowed in the club? We no longer have our own allotments.

A Mutual trading as a concept only applies to those activities which are organised and managed by the club on behalf of all the members. Individual transactions between members acting for themselves are simply sales; a contract is made between the seller and the buyer for produce, and the club has nothing to do with the contract which is made.

The only interest I can see for the club is in business being transacted on club premises. If your rules covered the sale of produce from the club's own allotments, this would be a different matter. But I see nothing wrong here.

6 Conduct outside the club

Q Can you tell us whether we are in order in expelling a member for conduct outside the club, but which is known to many of the members? Some say that it is only offences inside the club premises which can be used. Our club rules are not entirely clear on this.

A   It has long been a principle of members' clubs that they retain the right to accept or reject whoever they choose for membership. Recent legislation has attempted to change this in certain areas, but the principle of selection remains, for the most part, intact.

This being said, extreme care should always be taken in the method of removing persons from membership. The law gives them an equal right with all other members and an equal share in the club and expulsion should not be undertaken lightly.

There is no law which confines a club committee to consider actions within the club premises as the only ones on which to base expulsion. Your own rules merely say 'whose conduct, in the opinion of the committee, renders him unfit for membership...' This, in my view, can be taken to mean 'general conduct, inside or outside the club.' To ignore certain actions outside the club could lead to some unpleasant results.

But the most important point to bear in mind is that the committee will be acting as a form of court in deciding the issue. This means that they must be scrupulously fair in hearing evidence and appeals from the member concerned and other persons where necessary. Every opportunity must be given to the member to state his case, even if the evidence appears overwhelming. Only by doing this will you protect yourselves from the possibility of legal action in the future.

It is open to an expelled member to take action in the courts against a club which he feels has unfairly expelled him. A properly conducted enquiry will put the club on the right side of the law, even if others disagree with the final decision.

7 Banning order

Q   One of our members was expelled from the club for misconduct in 1997. He has made several applications for re-instatement, but has been turned down. Now, he has stated that under the Licensed Premises (Exclusion of Certain Persons) Act 1980 we must re-instate him, as the ban has been in effect for nearly five years. Can you advise us?

A   I am glad to say that this Act has nothing to do with the situation at your club, and would not affect this former member's rights in any way. This Act is more popularly known as the 'Ban the Thugs' Act and is only brought into effect by the courts. Where a person is actually convicted of violence or threatened violence on licensed premises, the court may issue an 'exclusion order' for any period up to three years.

It is entirely a matter for the discretion of the magistrates or judge who is trying the case. It is not always brought into effect, even in cases of proven violence.

The Act, however, only applies to licensed premises. It does not apply to clubs which are registered, as yours is.

Misconduct by a member is covered by your club rules, not by court decisions. It is up to your committee to decide, as fairly as possible, whether the conduct of a particular member, occurring inside or outside the club, renders him unfit for continuing membership. As long as you follow the procedure laid down in your rules, expulsion will be quite in order for serious cases.

After this, it is entirely up to your committee to decide about accepting the same person back. There is no time limit, except any minimum time laid down in your rules for re-application.

Many clubs fix such a minimum time so that there is a reasonable interval between refusal or expulsion and further consideration of the applicant.

If your committee have voted not to accept this further application, then they are quite in order. No-one can force you to take this man back if you do not wish to.

8 Lazy members

Q Could you advise us on the legality of including in our rules the expulsion of members who take no interest in the club, except to pick up dividends? Some of these people are members of other clubs and put nothing into the funds from which dividends are paid. We have 200 members and a waiting list of 40. We cannot let them in, owing to our ceiling of 200 by law.

A When you say that you are limited to 200 members 'by law' I must I assume that this is the maximum number of shareholders permitted under your present constitution. There is certainly no law which limits club membership to a maximum of 200 in a members' club. A change in the constitution seems appropriate.

In general, it is not possible to expel club members for laziness. There is no requirement of a general nature that club members should be active members, unless there is a rule to that effect. Such a rule, in order to be enforceable, would have to be couched in a positive way and not give some vague, arbitrary power to the committee.

Many clubs have a rule or byelaw governing the conduct of members of the committee. They are required to attend a minimum number of meetings in order to justify their continuing membership of that committee. Failure to attend without reasonable excuse renders them liable to removal.

I do not think that a similar rule could be found workable in the case of ordinary members. If the club had some ascertainable activity, such as a sports club, or the support of a particular project or charitable cause, then it would be possible for the rules to prescribe that members should actively participate, on pain of expulsion.

It would appear, however, that your club exists for mainly social purposes. This being the case, it is up to the individual members whether they wish to make use of the facilities or not. As long as they pay their subscription on time, there appears to be little you can do to compel them to use the club.

9 Torn dress

Q Recently a lady guest at our club caught her dress on a screwhead which was holding a panel. It had not been noticed. She is now asking for compensation, as the dress was only three weeks old. What are our legal obligations?

A As the lady in question was a guest, the club owes a duty of care to her. That duty extends to ensuring, as far as is reasonable, that she will come to no harm whilst on club premises.

The loose screw probably should have been rectified by a person acting on behalf of the club, and the club was technically negligent in allowing it to remain. I think she probably has a valid claim in the circumstances. The only matter open to debate is whether she herself contributed in any way to the damage.

If it was something which she could reasonably have foreseen, the club could

d guests attending a function. She is claiming that the club was responsible
' the loss and that she should be paid the full value of the coat. What is the
,al position?

It depends very much on whether 'the club' as such owes this member a
duty of care which it failed to exercise, i.e. whether the club as such was
responsible for the coat going missing. In this respect it is important to
nember the answer to question 6. The lady cannot sue herself.

It would appear that although there was no notice about articles left in the
»akroom, no money or other valuable consideration was rendered by her for the
vilege of leaving her coat there. She was not entitled to assume that the club
»uld take any more 'care' than was reasonable in the circumstances, to see that
: coat came to no harm. There was no subsequent contract made between the lady
ember and the club, such as a contract of bailment made by way of a fee for a
»akroom ticket, which might have affected the situation.

If negligence could be shown against a club servant, such as an attendant or
her member of the staff, then in certain circumstances an individual member
ight succeed in a claim. But there appears to be no active negligence or
relessness on anyone's part, through which the coat became lost. It would appear
it another person present at the event must have walked off with it — something
ich in the circumstances you describe the club could not possibly guard against.

2 Ban for life

We have had occasion to ban a member for a series of unsavoury
incidents culminating in an assault and fight on the premises. The
committee and a subsequent AGM put no time limit on the ban. The
an is now trying to have the ban lifted. What is the legal position. I enclose a
py of our club rules.

I note from your rules that they invest in the committee of the club power to
suspend or expel a member, after a hearing has been held. There is,
however, no mention of appeal or arbitration, which means that the matter is
emed to be in the hands of the club in general meeting.

It must be said that a club is deliberately an exclusive place, membership of
nich is limited or restricted in accordance with the rules. Persons may only be
troduced as members if they are found acceptable by the existing members, and in
me clubs the objection of just one member is sufficient to doom an application
ne famous 'black-ball' procedure for voting).

The courts will therefore not interfere in internal club matters unless a rank
justice is shown to have been done to an existing member which interferes with
s right to a great extent, or which goes against the club rules. However, if the club
s acted properly in expelling a member for gross misconduct, that expulsion may
st for life, if the club so desires.

The club is not required to fix a time limit for any form of disciplinary action
less the rules so provide (for example, in the case of a suspension, for 'up to six
onths'). Where a certain form of behaviour has made the person unacceptable to
e members in general, they may decide that the conduct is so bad as to render the
rson in question unfit ever to return. That is their prerogative, and the courts will
t interfere with that decision, as long as it is based on the rules.

Some clubs do allow an appeal from a suspension or expulsion to be heard by an
dependent arbitrator within a fixed time limit. However, where that time limit has

claim that her own negligence contributed to the damage, and would be
pay half the cost. But if the screw was not noticed by the club, then eq
not have been noticed by the guest.

The fact that you are a registered club does not affect this type
because the club as a whole is the occupier of the premises.

You should consider the question of adequate insurance cover as a r
incident, and also the posting up of a disclaimer notice at the entrance
This, while not absolving you from all liability, will afford some
protection in the light of any future claims.

10 Vote to allow back

Q Last year we had reason to expel three persons for pers
behaviour and foul language. They had been previously susp
now it is being suggested that when the committee change
immediately vote to allow them back in. I enclose a copy of our club
would like to know if this can be done and what we could do to stop i

A It would appear that there was a proper hearing before the commit
a vote in accordance with the rules it was decided to expel the
from the club. No time limit or date was given, but the three perso
appeal within the six month period allowed, so the matter did not reach ar

As far as reinstatement is concerned, this matter is not covered at a
rules. This is not surprising; few rules actually make any reference to rein
of expelled members, it being assumed that they would not wish to retur
members wish to have them back.

From your rules it would appear that any resolution of the committee
be rescinded if notice of the proposal is given at a previous meeting. Here
a problem. Is the penalty to be overturned, which is what rescinding the
will achieve? Or do the proposers really mean reinstatement after expulsi
is a different matter?

Whatever the proposal, there must be notice given of the intention to p
should not merely be raised at a subsequent committee meeting for in
debate. When it is known that certain persons wish the expelled memb
reinstated, it seems the most sensible course of action is for a specia
meeting of the club to be called, either by the committee or by those meml
wish the matter aired. This may be called under either one of two rules, a
be summoned by a 'person aggrieved' by a decision on a dispute about
ship.

It should be remembered that persons proposed for membership in the fi
have to have their names posted up in the club before they are elected. T
give any member who objects to the nomination a chance to put his view
election committee, who must seriously consider any such objection. This
more important in the case of reinstatement which should never be under
the face of strong opposition from existing members.

11 Lost coat in cloakroom

Q We have received a solicitor's letter on behalf of a lady memb
attends the club infrequently, but who lost her coat fro
cloakroom on a busy Saturday night when there were many m

expired, and the person merely wishes to be re-introduced to the club, then you are at liberty to refuse that request, however many times it is repeated.

13 Dispute on discipline

Q A serious problem has arisen in our club over the conduct of one long-standing member. He has refused to accept the decision of the committee that he should be suspended for three months and constantly enters the club with a group of friends. He claims that the committee have no power to suspend him and that the matter should be discussed at a meeting of members.

A I have studied your rules and although the question of disciplinary action is not covered in detail, it is clear that the committee retains the power to suspend or expel persons from membership. If this is the case, then decisions made by the committee are binding on all members and must be obeyed.

When this member joined the club he agreed to abide by its rules, including those covering disciplinary procedures. As long as the committee itself has acted properly in this matter, e.g. by giving the offending member an opportunity to explain his conduct, any subsequent decision which is taken by them should not be challenged.

I do not consider that the question of suspension should subsequently be referred to an extraordinary general meeting of members. There is no provision for this in your rules, although there is provision for arbitration in such matters. So the aggrieved member does have a further 'court of appeal' if he considers that your action was wrong.

Meanwhile it seems that your only recourse is to bring this again to his attention and threaten him with expulsion from the club if he continues to breach the rules in this way. Open defiance of a valid committee ruling could certainly be seen as grounds for expulsion. If this person still attempts to gain admittance, then the committee is within its rights to summon police assistance to have him ejected.

14 Temporary members

Q We have a special rule by which persons may be made temporary members of the club for the duration of their visit. My question is: what actual status do they have with regard to the facilities of the club? Can they play the gaming machines and play bingo and win the prizes, and can they enter 'members' only' competitions? I enclose our rules.

A From my study of your rules, it would appear that these temporary members enjoy all the rights and privileges of membership during their visit, except that they may not vote in meetings of the club, or stand for office.

This means that all other privileges are extended to them, except insofar as the rules curtail their activities in any way, which they do not appear to do. I can see nothing, therefore, to prevent such persons entering any competition or taking part in any gaming or other activity while they are on club premises.

Once they are permitted to participate, it is clear that they must also be allowed to win. You cannot ask people to lay out money by way of stakes or entrance fee and then subsequently prevent them from taking the prize, because of some technical lack of qualification. That would make the chances in the game less than equal, and would be in breach of the law.

It is entirely a matter for the members to decide how far they wish temporary membership to extend. I appreciate that if there is a long-running 'members-only' raffle, then it may be unfortunate if this is won by a person who is, to all intents and purposes, an 'outsider'. But the remedy is simple: restrict such raffles to ordinary members of the club only, thereby excluding temporary members from participation.

15 Members must obey steward's instruction

Q The committee of this club recently made new byelaws on the conduct of members while in the clubhouse and instructed the steward to enforce them. He is a full-time employee and not a club member. There is a feeling that only the elected chairman or secretary would have the power to ask a member to leave the clubhouse, or refuse service to him.

A Unless the rules limit the power to suspend a member specifically to named officials or individuals, there is no reason why such a measure should not be taken by someone other than the chairman or secretary. In particular, the secretary has no superior role to members of the committee. He is, in fact, their agent, to carry out whatever they determine at their meetings.

As far as staff are concerned, they may well be charged with ensuring that members abide by the club rules. This is for the benefit of the club as a whole. Each member agrees on joining to be bound by the rules which are in force, and it is part of his contract with the other members that he should continue to follow them.

The committee in your club appears to have a general power under the rules both to make byelaws and to suspend members for misconduct. This means that if they decide to enforce a certain rule or byelaw, as long as they give notice to the members and it is not in conflict with the rules (which byelaws can never be) then they have the power to do so.

They are also entitled to delegate this power for certain purposes. It seems to me perfectly in order for the club steward, who is placed in charge of the bar, to have certain authority delegated to him for the good conduct of that bar.

As an employee, appointed by the committee, he serves the interests of all the members. But this does not mean that all members have authority over him and that he cannot derive authority from another source.

If instructed by the committee, he may refuse to serve someone he considers in breach of a rule, or the law, and he may ask a member to leave if his conduct warrants it.

16 Abiding by arbitrator's decision

Q One of our members has been expelled twice for misconduct. His last expulsion finished and he applied for membership for the last two years, both of which were referred to the club's own elected arbitrators in accordance with the rules. Both applications were refused by them. But at our recent AGM a member proposed (without a seconder) that this former member be re-elected. After a vote he is now a member. It says in our rules that the arbitrators' decision shall be final, which I take to mean we cannot over-rule it, even at an AGM. Is this the case?

A   I agree that the procedure which was gone through at the meeting cannot possibly validate this man's re-election and it should be declared null and void.

It is essential for clubs to abide by arbitrators' decisions, whether they like them or not. This applies as much to internal arbitrators as it does to those outside the club who may be appointed in pursuance of a national scheme.

From time to time I receive complaints from clubs about arbitrators who do not accept the club's decision and find for the member. Yes, that would be nice, wouldn't it: offer an arbitration service on disputes which *always* came down on the side of the club?

But here is a case where the club **members** (or a small group of them) do not accept the arbitrators' decision. So one persons seeks to overturn it by the simple expedient of standing up at a general meeting. No notice, and no opportunity for anyone not there to know anything about what is being discussed.

That isn't democratic and it isn't what your rules provide, either. They state clearly that disputes will be resolved by arbitration, not by general meetings. Of course some people won't like it, but for the better running of the club, if you all submit to an arbitration system, then you *must* abide by it, or the system breaks down.

17 Share gives no absolute right

Q   We have recently purchased the freehold of our clubhouse. At a committee meeting last month, during a discussion on suspending or expelling a member, one committee person stated that each member was now a shareholder of the club and that we could not expel such a person. The only money members put up is their subscription for the year. Is there any truth in this claim?

A   Fortunately this is not true, as it would create an impossible situation in ordinary members' clubs. It is true that each member has a 'share' in the club and in some cases this share is real, by being issued to the person on election. Many workingmen's clubs have such a scheme, and their club is a kind of limited company. This is perhaps where your committee member got the idea from.

But there is an important extra ingredient — the club rules. On joining a club, each member agrees to be bound by the rules, and usually a copy of those rules is supplied to the joining member. Whether or not an actual share is issued, the contract between that member and the club involves agreeing to and complying with the rules.

Most, if not all, club rules cover the question of disciplinary procedures. In the case of Friendly Societies or Industrial and Provident Societies, where membership has some statutory rights involved, the question of suspension or expulsion is very carefully spelled out. Only after all the proper procedures have been followed can a shareholder be expelled and his share forfeited, and there is a procedure for appeal by an aggrieved member.

But none of this actually prevents a club from expelling a member/shareholder if the rules provide for it. This will apply not only to clubs which are incorporated in some way, but also to ordinary members' clubs who just operate with trustees. Where the committee has considered the bad conduct of a member, and has given that member a proper chance to explain his conduct, they can decide that he no longer is fit for membership and can remove it.

Chapter 11
The courts and the police

1 Work of court

Q I am very new to the club world and should like to ask what courts are involved with club law and administration and how do they operate? Do we have to take the oath before a judge?

A Applications concerning registered members' clubs such as yours are normally dealt with by the local magistrates' court, which sits throughout the year. Only in the case of an application for an occasional permission (*Chapter 13.13*) will you need to attend one of the licensing sessions, which are held on specific dates throughout the year.

Your attendance is sometimes required to answer one or two questions which the magistrates may have. There is no judge in attendance at this type of court. There will usually be three magistrates, sitting on 'the bench', the highest location in the court room, with the clerk sitting at a large table just below them. It is the clerk who will get the proceedings under way and will sometimes address you, although you should give your answers always to the chairman of the magistrates, who sits in the centre chair.

Appearing in a court can be quite frightening at the best of times, particularly when it is normally used for criminal cases. However, the magistrates are used to seeing persons making applications for licences, certificates and other permissions, and they usually take such matters first, before the normal criminal proceedings get under way.

You will be called to the witness stand and asked to take the oath to tell the truth. This is a usual procedure and in no way suggests that you are about to lie, or are to be charged with an offence!

Matters normally take only a few minutes, especially where uncomplicated issues are concerned. In the case of most registered clubs, renewals and other applications are done administratively by the court office and there is no need to appear. If, however, there is an objection to something which the club wishes to do, you will receive notification of this and the matter may be adjourned to give you more time to seek legal advice and assistance.

For licensed clubs, the procedure is similar to that for public house licensees. Appearances are usually at the licensing sessions, if required, although initially you may be required to go before the magistrates for a protection order for the club, prior to the transfer of the licence.

Only where there is an appeal against a decision of the magistrates or the licensing justices will the matter go to a higher court, known as the Crown Court. Here, both a judge and magistrates will sit, and the club will normally be represented by counsel or a solicitor.

2 Following procedure

Q Someone has told me that the magistrates now follow a Good Practice Guide in their dealings with registered clubs. What does this mean and how does it affect us?

A The magistrates who handle all licensing and club matters, together with the Justices' Clerks' Society, produced a *Good Practice Guide* in 1999, to bring more consistency to the way licences and certificates were dealt with.

It has made a difference. The main one is that there are fewer occasions when people are asked to turn up in court, there is slightly more paperwork as a result, with additional questionnaires to fill in and send back and there seems to be slightly less flexibility in the way clubs are dealt with.

For example, the *Guide* suggests that registration certificates should be renewed for five years instead of the maximum of ten, which has been usual in the past. This has caused surprise to some clubs, who find that their renewal certificate is made out for the shorter time, even though they expected a full ten-year period.

The questionnaires, too, delve into such things as the presence of children, their consumption of liquor, hiring of club premises, voting rights of members, the rights of guests and visitors and the purposes of the club. This must be returned to the clerk prior to the hearing of the renewal and is in addition to the actual application form itself.

The *Guide* itself explains the law on children and young persons in clubs, voting rights under schedule 7, supply of liquor to non-members, guests and visitors and '*The Little Ship Club* rule' (*see Chapter 18*). It is revised annually and a new edition is issued at the beginning of the year in time for the Annual Licensing Sessions in February.

Copies of the *Guide* can be obtained from the Justices' Clerks' Society at the address in Appendix D.

3 Increased drinking

Q As a result of improving the accommodation at this licensed club, I wish to extend the lounge bar and create a residents' bar as well. Do I have to do anything about my licence when I have finished the work?

A It is no good waiting until after the work has been carried out to contact the justices. You must do it before you even start. As yours is a proprietary club, you operate under a justices' licence. This means that any structural alterations which you intend to make to the licensed part of the premises require the prior consent of the licensing bench.

The accommodation improvements, I assume, were carried out after the relevant planning consent had been obtained from the local authority. As this residential area is outside the scope of the licence, there was at that time no requirement to consult the justices.

But this plan for the bar areas is different. Although it would appear that you do not intend to change or extend the bars themselves, you are giving increased facilities for drinking, and this brings the licensing laws into operation.

The Licensing Act clearly states that any alteration which increases the facilities for drinking requires the prior consent of the justices. They will want to see a plan of the relevant parts of the club, together with details of what structural or other work is intended. Only after they have consented, or made recommendations for changes, can the work start.

It is clear that this section of the Act affects proprietary clubs as well as public houses, whether the licence is issued under section 1 or section 55 of the Act. However, it does no apply to registered members' clubs, unless the alterations are so fundamental as to create an entirely new club which might require re-registration (*see next question*).

The penalty for failure to obtain prior permission is heavy. The court can either order you to restore the premises to their original condition, or order you to forfeit the licence entirely. So it is best to wait until the next licensing sessions and gain the justices' approval first.

4 Notifying clerk of changes

Q We have recently completed an extension to our clubhouse and I have informed the secretary that he must immediately notify the clerk to the justices to have the registration certificate altered. He says this is not necessary. Could you please adjudicate?

A Your secretary is right. There is no immediate requirement to notify the local court of any extension of the type you describe. There is a complete difference between registered clubs and licensed premises in this respect. In the case of pubs, they require prior approval from the licensing justices for any alterations or extensions to their premises (other than private, unlicensed areas).

No such approval or re-registration is legally required for clubs. The only notification to the court which is required by law is when the registration certificate itself comes up for renewal.

Where the alteration does not involve a complete change of the character of the club or its premises and is simply an extension of the facilities at the same address, there is nothing in the Licensing Act which requires approval from the court. The only requirement is for the club to obtain prior planning consent from the local authority, if the alteration involves enough of the property to make this necessary.

It must be remembered that registration merely confers upon the club the right to supply liquor to its members and their guests. It does not specify the areas of the club where such liquor may be dispensed, or the nature of the bar or bars from which it is supplied.

Under section 52 of the Licensing Act 1964, a certificate 'may' be varied on application by the club during its currency, in respect of 'different, additional or enlarged premises'. But it is not a requirement that this is done in the case of extensions to the existing building.

It should also be remembered that an application under this section does not even extend the life of the certificate. It still needs renewal at the same time as if the notification has not been given, even though in some cases the complete renewal procedure has to be complied with at that time.

It makes more sense to wait until the time of renewal to acquaint the court with the changes which have taken place.

QUESTIONS & ANSWERS ON CLUB LAW

5 Authority for sports ground bar

Q We have just completed the modernisation of our sports ground pavilion, which is some distance from the company headquarters. Currently we hold a registration certificate in respect of the club bar at the works, but we do not hold one for the sports ground. We intend to install a bar in the new lounge/hall at the pavilion and wonder whether we have to apply for a separate registration for this?

A You do not have to apply for separate registration if you already hold a certificate for the club and it is the same club which intends to run the bar at the sports ground under its existing rules.

Under section 52 of the Licensing Act 1964, a single registration certificate may relate to any number of premises of the same club. The certificate may also be varied, either at the time of renewal or otherwise, as regards the premises to which it relates.

Nor is it a requirement that the premises must be in the same local authority or licensing area to qualify for inclusion. There is provision in the Licensing Act for the clerk to notify both the police and the local authority in the 'new' area that you intend to apply.

What you have to do is to study the rules in Schedule 6 to the Licensing Act 1964, which apply to the issue or renewal of a registration certificate. You may do this directly or by using the club solicitor, which in my view would be the wiser course.

The application, as is usual, must be signed by the chairman or secretary of the club and sent to the magistrates' clerk, together with the additional copies he needs to send on to the other persons mentioned above. He will let you know how many he needs.

Secondly, you will have to display a notice on or near the pavilion for seven days after the application, so that the public can read it. You must also take an advertisement in a newspaper which circulates in that area, stating that the application is being made.

If the court decides that the application is straightforward and there are no objections, it may grant the variation without a hearing. None of this will affect the validity of your current certificate and even if the application for the pavilion is refused, your club bar will continue.

The registration certificate will continue in force for as long as it is scheduled to last at present, at which time you will renew the single certificate for both sets of premises.

6 Rule changes must be notified

Q A colleague has told me that you have to write to the justices' clerk whenever you change a rule or a byelaw. I thought it was only when you altered your permitted hours or applied for renewal of registration. Is this true?

A There is no requirement to notify the magistrates' clerk directly about ordinary changes in the rules, and certainly not changes in byelaws, which are for internal administration only. However, section 48 of the Licensing

Act 1964 makes it obligatory for clubs to notify the chief officer of police and the clerk to the local authority, in writing, within 28 days of a rule change being made.

It is a duty which falls specifically to the secretary of the club, who may be fined up to £200 for his failure to make this notification.

Where there is any change in the particulars of the club which are entered in the register of clubs kept by the clerk to the magistrates, or any change in the permitted hours fixed by the club, then either the chairman or the secretary may sign the notice which must be sent to this official. The fine for failure to make this notification is anything up to £1000).

If the permitted hours for Christmas Day are enshrined in the rules (which they should not be) then any change will require a notification to all three officials. If the permitted hours are contained in the byelaws, only the magistrates' clerk will require notice.

This is not to say that rule changes may be vetoed by the court or the police, except where they conflict with the law, or where they authorise sales of liquor which the court has expressly forbidden.

Clubs which are registered under the Friendly Societies or Industrial and Provident Societies Acts must also formally notify the Financial Services Authority (FSA) of any changes in rules and these will not be effective until so registered.

7 Reducing numbers

Q Recently, it has been suggested to our committee by the local clerk that we reduce the number of our members from 600 to around 450. I am at a loss to explain this demand. Can you tell me whether this is legally possible?

A You say that this is a suggestion from your local clerk. I take it you mean the magistrates' clerk, and that you are a registered members' club. I take it also that this was by way of a suggestion rather than a demand.

I can find no reason for a clerk to seek a reduction in actual membership from a club. I can certainly see the sense in a fire authority or safety officer recommending a maximum number of persons who may be on the premises at any one time, but this has nothing to do with the total membership on the register.

The actual membership of a club often bears little or no relationship to the use of the premises. Many community clubs have a membership list running into thousands. Some clubs formed for housing estates have the electoral register as their membership list! But there are only a handful of regular users in many of these clubs.

Some clubs, as a matter of policy, restrict or close their membership. This is perfectly in order. So is creating a waiting list for new members. If members are to enjoy the facilities to the full it seems sensible not to crowd the membership list.

But once a person has been accepted into membership, he or she cannot be 'removed' on a casual whim. There must be valid reasons under the rules for expulsion from membership. Bad conduct, or failure to pay subscriptions due, could mean termination of membership. But it would not be lawful to refuse to accept a renewal of subscription in order to reduce numbers.

Any person prohibited from making use of a members' club without a good reason may have recourse to the courts, to claim his rights. There have been several instances of successful actions of this type by aggrieved members.

8 Magistrates' powers

Q I have recently taken over as chairman of this club and find the rules very strict in certain respects; in particular, they state that no changes may be made to membership classes and to social club provision 'without the prior consent of the justices'. Is this the normal practice for club rules these days?

A I should make it clear that the magistrates have no power at all to dictate actual rules to clubs. They have certainly exceeded their authority in your case, because neither of the rules they have insisted on is legally necessary for a registered club.

Now that they have been included, of course, the bench will hold that they must be complied with. My own view is that they should be removed as soon as possible.

Any restrictions which a court wishes to place on the operation of a registered members' club should be made part of the certificate of registration itself. Then, if the club finds the requirements too onerous it may use the ordinary machinery of court procedure to seek to have changes made.

But the magistrates have no blanket authority over club rules. They are entitled to look at the rules to see if they comply in certain important respects with schedule 7 to the Licensing Act 1964. But schedule 7 is by no means binding and clubs which do not exactly conform are still entitled, after due consideration to receive and retain registration.

The magistrates are also given the power under section 49 of the Act to limit the admission of non-members (except inter-affiliated visitors and certain other classes). But they should then impose a condition on the certificate of registration, not directly into the club rules.

They certainly have no right to control membership classes, or the hours during which the club is to be open. These are clearly the province of the club committee.

9 Conditions should be challenged

Q We have recently been granted a renewal of our club registration certificate subject to a number of conditions, including a total ban on persons under 18 and a limit on the number of people allowed into the club for events. These conditions were imposed on the recommendation of the clerk and I should like to know what power he has to do this?

A As I wrote in the previous answer, there is no specific authority under the Licensing Act 1964 for the magistrates to impose conditions on a certificate of registration, other than those laid down in the Act.

This is in direct contrast to the situation with regard to liquor licences generally. The licensing justices do have the power to impose conditions on a licence, by virtue of section 4 of the Act. There is no similar provision for clubs, and it seems clear that none was intended by Parliament.

It is interesting that you should mention the clerk's role in this matter. Legally, of course, he has no authority to undertake the role of the magistrates, or to forestall their discretion. Even after the publication of the *Good Practice Guide*, I continue to receive reports of clerks acting as their own registration authority, often without reference to the bench. While it is appreciated that clerks have an intimate working knowledge of the law which they administer, clubs should not thereby assume that everything which they say cannot be challenged.

Your own example is a case in point. There is absolutely no authority for the inclusion of a condition on your registration certificate banning persons under 18 from the club. Indeed, this particular point has been satisfactorily dealt with in the High Court and was well publicised at that time. The bench has no power to impose such a ban, or to limit membership of such a club to persons over 18, because that is not provided for in the Licensing Act, and admitting younger members is perfectly legal.

The other point about a limitation of numbers again appears to have no statutory authority. The magistrates are not the entertainment licensing authority for clubs, which are not usually required to hold an entertainment licence at all. The condition which you have sent to me appears to be a direct transfer from entertainment licensing, which is now the province of the local authority and not the magistrates.

My suggestion is that both these conditions should be challenged by the club, because they appear to me to be beyond the proper powers of the magistrates on renewing a registration certificate.

10 Fire safety shock

Q We have recently applied for renewal of our 10-year registration, well in advance, I might say. The first thing I was informed was that renewal would only be for five years, as this was now 'policy'. The second shock was that the fire authority have sent a long and detailed letter of structural and other improvements to the premises which they say must be carried out. This will cost a great deal of money. Is there anything we can do to fight this?

A Under the terms of the Licensing Act 1964, a copy of the application for renewal of a registration certificate must be sent on by the court clerk to both the police and the fire authority. This means that the fire officers can invoke section 46 of the Act, both to inspect the premises and subsequently to object to the renewal, if they feel so inclined.

As the last time your premises were inspected was ten years ago, it may be that the general guidelines for premises such as yours which the fire authority use have been changed. Certainly, the Home Office issues guidelines for the safety of places of entertainment and like premises, and these could well be used as the basis for recommendations on safety precautions for a club of your size.

There is always greater concern about safety in premises where large numbers of people congregate, whether they be private or public places. Inspection of registered club premises is comparatively rare, so the fire officers may take greater pains, knowing that they may be unable to come back for five years or more.

You may be able to compromise on certain elements of this document if you are prepared to discuss it with the fire officer concerned. If you fail to reach full agreement on what needs to be done, then you can proceed to a hearing of the application and put your points to the magistrates. If they refuse the renewal, you can take the matter on to the Crown Court by way of appeal.

On the other matter you raise, there is no obligation on the magistrates to renew a certificate for the same period as it was granted previously, but there would have to be good reasons why it should be curtailed. Certainly, a court official cannot amend your application to five years, if you have requested ten. That is your right under the Licensing Act.

11 Police access to members' club

Q Can you tell me under what circumstances the police are allowed entry to this ex-service club? We have not had any problem, but I am a new secretary and want to be sure of the legal position.

A It is very sensible to be wise **before** the event rather that after it! You have enclosed your rules which show me that you are a registered members' club, not operated under a licence. In such circumstances the police do not have an automatic right of access, and none is given to them under the terms of the Licensing Act 1964.

In most circumstances, therefore, they would have to request admission from an officer of the club and could not enter on a routine visit by demanding entry on the door.

There are only two circumstances under which police are given a statutory right of entry to a members' club. The first is where the club operates a special hours certificate. Police are allowed access from the end of 'normal' hours, that is, from 11 pm until half an hour after the terminal hour on the certificate (*see Chapter 16 for further details*).

The second is where the club has obtained an occasional permission, allowing members of the public to be served. These are limited to 12 occasions in any period of 12 months. The police have access for the duration of the permission and it is an offence to refuse to admit them.

The police are not given authority to inspect gaming machine permits or other items 'on the spot', and a formal request should always be made of the secretary in such cases. Other authorities, such as Customs & Excise and health officials, **do** have a statutory right of entry, but they would normally ask to see the secretary or other club officer.

12 Police objections to special hours

Q Can you tell me what rights the police have with regard to objecting to our special hours certificate or the use of the premises for musical events and special festivals? They have suggested that they can cut back my hours to normal pub hours, so that we cannot have any late events, due to rowdyism, which has never been a problem here.

A The police in certain areas do seem to have embarked on a campaign against late opening, particularly of clubs. They use the powers given to them under the Licensing (Amendment) Act 1980, which came into force in October 1982, and also by the recent case of *Shipley*.

Under the additional section 81A of the Licensing Act 1964, the police may apply to the licensing justices (or in the case of registered clubs, the magistrates) to restrict the hours allowed under a special hours certificate to a time earlier than 2 am (or 3 am in London).

They have to convince the bench either that (a) the genuine use of the premises for providing music and dancing does not last until the end of the extension, or (b) curtailing the hours will avoid or reduce any disturbance to or annoyance of residents in the neighbourhood of the premises, and might also prevent the occurrence of disorderly conduct in the premises.

In addition to this, of course, they retain the overall right to object to the renewal of the certificate as a whole, on the grounds of ill-conducted premises or nuisance, which would have the effect of reducing the permitted hours to normal hours for the district.

If they apply for the restriction first mentioned above, then the court may impose a condition on the certificate, specifying the time when the permitted hours will end. This can be any time between midnight and the statutory terminal hour; in practice it is likely to be fixed at either midnight or 1 am.

You are entitled to appeal against the imposition of the restriction, and also to ask subsequently for the condition to be removed.

Clearly, it is best if you can avoid the restriction entirely, by making your own representations to the bench that you have been unfairly singled out when your own premises are well conducted and do not cause disturbance.

The police do not always achieve what they set out for, and some benches dislike any 'blanket' policy over late-night opening. So it may be that in your case no action will be taken. But you must prepare your arguments well, in case there is an objection.

13 Police log of complaints

Q Throughout the year we have had a number of incidents, and I have always contacted the police whenever necessary. Now, I hear that they can use their own records of these calls for assistance to object at the renewal of my club licence. Surely this, and anonymous telephone calls, are unfair as evidence against the licensee?

A The police log each and every incoming call asking for assistance or reporting incidents. They do this as a matter of course, and every call has to be recorded. But wherever possible they also record the name of the caller and the reason for the call.

It should be remembered that any licensee has the statutory right to summon assistance from the police if a customer is drunk, violent, quarrelsome or disorderly. In such circumstances they can actually demand that a police constable should assist in removing the unwanted person. It is not merely a request but a statutory right to assistance.

In such circumstances the police record should be clear and should state that the licensee summoned help. As this is a right, it can hardly be used against the licensee in seeking to object to renewal.

As far as anonymous calls are concerned, the police decide on whether the call should be taken seriously (some are obviously cranks or drunks), and often find that genuine calls are made in this way by people not wishing to be identified. With clubs the most common complaint is late night noise and the most common reason for not identifying the caller is fear of reprisal or victimisation.

Although you must take any objection from neighbours seriously, it is not advisable to become obsessed with the possibility of objections to the licence. Many callers who refuse to give their name will certainly not turn up in court to object, and the police will only formally oppose you if other methods have entirely failed.

In any case, you will receive extra time to prepare your case to counter any objections raised in court. If objections to renewal are not notified in writing in advance of the hearing they cannot be entertained, but if proper objections are received, the justices usually adjourn the hearing.

14 Police do not renew

Q Some time ago we notified the police about the renewal of our registration, as they handle all our extensions and licensing matters here. We asked them if there would be any objections and they said there would be no problem, so we left the matter. Now we find that we still have to make a further application and that we are too late to do this. What will happen?

A You have made the mistake of assuming that matters to do with registration and the supply of liquor are dealt with directly by the local police. This is not the case; you must apply to the magistrates' court in the case of renewal of registration (*see Chapter 6.10*).

I think this has come about because in the London area the police do have an administrative responsibility for extensions to permitted hours. Therefore, if your club wants an extension for a special event, I expect that you contact a named officer at your local police station and give him the details. The police will also convey to you from time to time the general feelings of the justices with regard to late-night drinking, extensions and the like.

What appears to have happened is that you have failed to give the required 28 days' notice to the magistrates of your intention to renew the registration, in which case the old registration certificate will expire and you will have to stop serving intoxicating liquor until it is renewed.

In Scotland, clubs in your position are entitled to throw themselves on the mercy of the Registrar, and if he is satisfied that the failure to lodge the application within the correct time was due to 'inadvertence', he can still entertain it. However, in England if the registration has entirely expired, there will still be a full 28-day 'dry' period.

Some clubs have succeeded in obtaining the services of a local licensee to apply for an occasional licence to cover this period while the application goes through.

15 Agents provocateurs

Q I have heard this expression used in relation to police activities with regard to registered members' clubs and I should be grateful if you could explain exactly what is meant and how do the police operate?

A This is something of an emotive issue, not only among clubs but also within the police force, where such a phrase is understandably disliked. In simple terms, it means that plain-clothes officers attempt to prove that the club is either breaking the law or not operating correctly by posing as members of the public and seeking to use the facilities of the club.

The reason for this type of under-cover action lies in the private nature of members' clubs. Police do not have a right of entry, except in certain limited cases described in this chapter. They can, in fact, be refused entry on the door of the club, unless they have a warrant or other authority to enter. This means that, in their terms, supervision of club activities is very difficult.

The main problem in this type of activity occurs if it is claimed that officers did not tell the exact truth in order to gain admission. For example, if they claimed to be members of an affiliated club, or guests of an existing member (both of which statements, if true, would have allowed them entry under the correct procedures) and then subsequently charged the club with permitting members of the public to gain admission and play the gaming machines.

In the eyes of the club, they were not members of the public, and had they been so they would have been refused entry. But it may be that an insufficient check on their claimed credentials was made on the door, with the result that unqualified persons did gain entry.

As a result of the bad publicity surrounding actions of this type, most police forces tend to rely on observation, information and eventually admission by warrant where they suspect that a club is operating illegally.

16 Police power to close

Q I have heard that police now have power to close down licensed premises on the spot for rowdy behaviour and also for noise, including music. Is this true and does it apply to licensed clubs?

A The new police powers contained in the Criminal Justice and Police Act 2001 have been added to the Licensing Act 1964, giving power to a senior police officer of the rank of inspector or above to issue a closure order against 'relevant licensed premises'.

These will include public houses and licensed clubs, but will not include off-licences, registered members' clubs, theatres or premises for which an occasional licence is in force.

As yours is a licensed club, you are indeed vulnerable to an order being made against you, which will require you to stop serving immediately and to take all possible steps to remove customers from the premises for the duration of the order (which can be anything up to 24 hours).

You are also right that in addition to rowdy behaviour and disturbance to neighbours by customers, the police action could be triggered by loud music emanating from the premises, although this is more usually the province of the local environmental health department. It is very likely in such circumstances that you will be contacted in advance and told about the noise and given an opportunity to reduce the volume or stop the music before closure action is taken.

The actual closure order triggers off a train of events which will lead you to an appearance before the justices to discuss whether or not your licence should be revoked. If you have complied immediately with the order and have taken steps to reduce or eliminate noise or disturbance, however, it may be that the justices will permit you to keep the licence. It is only in serious cases of repeated disturbance and lack of co-operation that the revocation will go ahead.

You cannot appeal directly against a closure order, but you can appeal against any subsequent decision made by the justices, which could include keeping your club shut for a period of time. But it would be far better to avoid any chance of this occurring by ensuring that you have a good working relationship with the police and do not allow excessive noise from your premises.

Chapter 12
Running the bar

1 Franchise for bar

Q My committee is considering whether to put the bar operation of this club out to franchise and we would welcome your advice on this matter.

A I would suggest that you take both legal and financial advice before committing yourselves to any agreement which will bind the club. You must also carefully consider what it is you are trying the achieve by this, in terms of the viability of the club.

At first sight, it would appear that the idea is a non-starter, from the legal point of view. Section 41 of the Licensing Act 1964 covers the qualifications for registration and I note that your club is currently also registered under the Industrial and Provident Societies Acts. It is clear that to exist as a genuine members' club, the affairs ought to be run by the members themselves.

Under section 41, a club is only qualified to receive a registration certificate if, among other things:

'Intoxicating liquor is not supplied, or intended to be supplied, to members on the premises otherwise than on behalf of the club;

also

'that the purchase and supply of intoxicating liquor should be managed by an elective committee and that no arrangements are made or intended to be made for any person to derive financial benefit from the supply of intoxicating liquor to members and guests'.

As I understand it, a franchise system means that an operating company pays a straight fee to the club funds and then operates the bars and takes the profits. The club ceases to have an everyday administrative control over bar stocks, bar funds and profit margins, the employment of staff and the payment of wages.

This would, in my view, destroy one of the essential characteristics of a registered members' club, and would certainly require a re-think of the authority to supply liquor, probably requiring a licence rather than a certificate.

If that is the course you wish to take, then the club constitution would also have to be altered, with attendant problems over the registration of the club itself as an industrial and provident society. On the facts which you have supplied to me, I do not think this is a good idea at all.

2 Drinking-up time

Q Who in the club is responsible for ensuring that drinking-up time is adhered to? Is it entirely the steward's responsibility, or is it the secretary or committee? I feel that, as steward. I am in a difficult position and would welcome your guidance.

A The most important point is that drinking-up time is legally binding on registered clubs in exactly the same way as public houses. Clubs are in no special position in this respect, and the 20-minute rule applies strictly on any period of permitted hours, even if the club is not physically closing its doors at that time.

The second important point is that the offence contained in the Licensing Act is 'consuming liquor outside permitted hours.' So the main offender is the member who continues to drink after the concessionary period.

The only offence with which you could be charged as steward is in 'aiding and abetting' persons to consume liquor. The prosecution would have to show that you made no attempt to collect glasses or to persuade members to drink up, or turned a blind eye to their breaking the law.

It is even more difficult to prosecute a steward for this offence, because of his position as an employee of the club. If at the time of the alleged offence, members of the committee were present, then it would seem appropriate that they should face the court, as the persons responsible for ensuring compliance with the licensing laws.

If, for example, a member refuses to hand over his glass to you, there is nothing you can do to prevent him breaking the law, short of using force, which you are not required to do. I do not know whether your contract of employment requires you in general terms to comply with the licensing laws, but if you are dissatisfied with members' reactions at closing time, then you must bring it up with the secretary or committee and ensure that it is noted, so that it cannot rebound on you later.

3 Outside drinks

Q Is it true that it is illegal for members to take drinks outside the club in an open vessel, and they must be served with closed bottles for such purposes?

A This is not the legal position at all, and for a club such as yours, with its own sports ground. I should have thought that the point was a vital one. A registration certificate (or a licence, for that matter) authorises a club to supply drinks to its members, and on their order to guests, at the premises for which the registration has been sought.

It also authorises the club to make that same supply at any premises or place which the club is using on a special occasion for the accommodation of members and guests.

Although in some circles the words 'premises' have been taken to mean buildings, it is clear that in this context the expression 'club premises' means the buildings and the adjoining sportsfield, all of which are under the control of the sports club.

It would be impracticable and unenforceable for the club members to be compelled to confine their drinking to one area of the club, particularly during the summer months.

The committee and bar staff have a duty to ensure that consumption of liquor ceases on club premises at the correct time, according to the club's permitted hours. The club may also make byelaws and regulations preventing members taking drinks to certain places. Obvious examples are the squash courts and the swimming pool.

Apart from an internal regulations, however, there is nothing in law to prevent persons taking drinks from the bar to another place for consumption.

With regard to your other point, again there is nothing in law to force members to take closed bottles out of the bar. For take-home supplies this would seem to be a matter of practicality, rather than law. But for drinking on the premises, most members would prefer the bar staff to do the work for them!

4 Stamped measures not needed

Q At a recent event, we used disposable plastic tumblers for drinks which were to be taken outside. Someone who was a guest of a member commented that this was not legal, as we had to serve beer in properly stamped glasses. Is this true?

A It is clear from your rules and constitution, which you have enclosed, that you are a members' club operating under a certificate of registration. This means that you are exempt from the relevant legislation covering the measures to be used for intoxicating liquor, including glasses for beer and cider, or measuring instruments for certain spirits.

Many members confuse the rules for clubs with those of public houses. The regulations apply only to 'sale by retail'. It has been long established that this term does not cover the transaction in a members' club, which is merely the re-distribution of the club stock among the members themselves. They already own a share in the liquor, so it is not 'sold' to them.

Both the regulations for beer/cider and those for spirits will apply to proprietary clubs, operating under some form of justices' licence, because they do sell to their members. But registered clubs do not, although most will comply, in order to maintain proper stock control.

5 Drinks on credit

Q Can you tell me whether the law on credit for drinks applies in a members' club or not? One of the senior members of the committee ran up a 'slate' with the relief steward while I was on holiday. Although he paid the secretary direct at the weekend, he now wants to continue the practice with me. As steward, what should I do?

A You must refuse his request and report the situation to the club secretary. What this committee member proposes is in direct contravention of the Licensing Act 1964, and you are entitled to make this known to your employers.

It should be remembered that members of a club's committee enjoy no special privileges at the club bar, and are not entitled to instruct the steward personally on such matters. If this person insists on not paying and tries to give you instruction based on his personal position within the club, you must still insist on payment, because you may be personally liable under the Act.

Section 166 specifically states that no person shall, in any licensed premises or the premises of a registered club sell or supply liquor on credit, or consume intoxicating liquor unless it has been paid for at the time.

A promise to pay the money later is not sufficient. There must actually be a transaction between the persons in charge of the bar and the ''customer''. This means a transfer of money or money's worth (such as a cheque or credit card).

This condition does not affect situations where the club supplies drinks free of charge, or has made a special arrangement with persons to receive drinks at the expense of the club funds. Nor does it affect the situation where one member pays in advance for a drink for another member, to be ordered and consumed later. The steward accepts the money in advance and the drink is thereby 'paid for' at the time when it is supplied.

6 Bottles behind bar

Q We make a number of off-sales in our club and it has been my practice to look after these for members on a shelf behind the bar. When the member is about to leave he asks for his bottles etc and takes them home. Someone has told me that you have said this is illegal after time. Can you explain?

A There are two important points to be borne in mind concerning off sales — the position of the club and the position of the member on his way home. The Licensing Act states that it is illegal, except during the permitted hours, to 'sell or supply to any person...in premises in respect of which a club is registered any intoxicating liquor, whether to be consumed on or off the premises...'

The word 'supply' in this context can mean two things. It can mean the transaction between a club and a member, which in law is not a sale; or it can mean the passing over of drink already paid for but not claimed.

The fact that money has changed hands before the end of permitted hours does not subsequently legalise the supply of liquor after hours. If that were the case, members could order three or four pints before 'time' and then claim them after the bell. This, as you know, is not the legal position.

All service of drink should cease at the terminal hour, and members are allowed ten minutes to consume drinks already supplied to them, or to take their off-sales away from the premises. At the end of the 20-minute period, further consumption becomes illegal. So does taking liquor away from the premises.

It follows that persons with off-sales (strictly speaking, in a members' club these should be called 'off-supplies') should leave the premises before the end of drinking-up time, because as soon as they get outside they may be apprehended by the police if the 20-minute period has elapsed.

In such cases the club will not necessarily be charged with any offence. But the police might suspect that supplies are being made after time, which could result in a raid in the future.

As far as the paid-for bottles are concerned, these must be collected before time, and a notice to that effect should be placed behind the bar, to ensure compliance with the law. If a member then comes to the bar after time and asks for his bottles, it would be illegal to supply them. He should, strictly speaking, wait until the next period of permitted hours before he can take them from the premises.

7 Price list

Q Is it a legal requirement for all clubs to display a price list and must it be displayed in a prominent position? One regular club member says we can be prosecuted if we do not display our prices at all times.

A Price lists for food and drink are required on certain premises. The law was changed in 1979 so that it is not now obligatory to list every item of food and drink which is available—just a representative sample. But most establishments find it more convenient to list their whole range at some point in the premises, or on a menu.

But the Price Marking (Food and Drink on Premises) Order 1979 does *NOT* apply to '. . . premises on which food is ordinarily supplied . . . only to members of a bona fide club or their guests . . .'

Because of the wording of that particular sentence, I would take this exemption to apply to all types of genuine clubs where access is restricted. Thus, proprietary clubs and night clubs which operate as genuine clubs can also escape the provisions of the Order.

This being said, a price list can assist both members and staff, even though it is not legally necessary. It saves any argument over the prices charged and also can cut down on the temptation for bar staff to 'fiddle' the total.

8 Lined glasses

Q One of our members has brought up the question of lined glasses for draught beer. He insists that we should use these in our club, rather than brim measures. In fact, we have not bothered too much with the style or type of glasses in the past. Is it legally necessary for us to go to the expense of switching to these glasses?

A Your member is quite wrong. There is no requirement for any establishment which serves draught beer to have lined glasses available. In fact. it would appear that any new law on the matter has now been officially discounted.

In any case, it would not affect registered clubs. They are not bound by the provisions of the Weights and Measures Act 1985 with regard to measurement and are not in law required to have stamped glasses at all.

This is not widely publicised, because the majority of glasses and spirit measures now comply with the general law. But it may at some stage be important for clubs to realise their exemption.

For example, certain representatives may try and sell the club expensive measuring equipment on the understanding that it is legally required. Club officials may unwittingly spend a great deal of money in complying with a law from which they are exempt!

Lined glasses have the merit of giving a full pint with room for the head as well. They may result in satisfied members, but it should be remembered that their use can lead to over-pouring and an adjustment of allowances and/or margins.

Where beer is metered at the source, often in the cellar, over-sized glasses are useful to avoid any spillage. Stock control is also guaranteed, as the equipment will dispense only a full half of beer and cannot pour too much. In fact, the member is guaranteed a full pint or half-pint of liquid, without any dispute as to the size of the head!

9 Youngsters' shandy

Q Recently there was a heated debate between one of our members and the club steward, and I suggested I would write to you for a ruling. The steward refuses to allow children to consume shandy made from the pump. He says he has read that this is illegal, and they must have bottled shandy. Our member says he is wrong. Can you help us?

A The general position is that children under the age of 18 are not allowed to consume alcohol in the bar of licensed premises. This would include a 'made' shandy where the beer was poured from the pump, but not a bottled shandy, which is pre-packed with an alcoholic strength not exceeding 1.2 per cent.

That rule does not apply to clubs, where persons under the age of 18 are not prohibited by law from consuming alcohol. However, they must qualify for entry to the club in some way, either as members or guests. Otherwise they are merely members of the public.

If the club rules prohibit supply or consumption of liquor to or by persons under 18, then these should be observed. But if your rules do not cover the point, there is nothing illegal in allowing youngsters to consume made shandy in the bar.

10 Off-sales to guests

Q What is the law on people taking off-sales away from a members' club? I thought this was illegal, but one of our committee says that anyone can take off-sales, even guests, if they have been properly admitted to the premises.

A The supply of liquor for consumption off the premises (which in the case of a members' club is not a 'sale' but a 'supply') is governed by section 39 of the Licensing Act 1964.

That section makes it perfectly clear that such supplies may only be made to a member in person. This means that no guest or visitor may be allowed to make a purchase for consumption off the premises, and that no-one who is not a member may be sent to the club in order to fetch liquor on behalf of a member.

This makes illegal the practice of sending another member of the family to bring home liquor, unless the 'messenger' is also a member of the club authorised to be supplied with liquor in his or her own right.

As in the case of normal bar trading, the supply of drinks to take home may only be made during the permitted hours which operate in the club. No such supply may be made outside those hours, and no one may leave the club during non-permitted hours with liquor which has been supplied there.

However, if the club arranged for the dispatch of liquor which had been ordered while the bar was open, then the delivery could take place during non-permitted hours, as long as it was transported by the club and not carried by the member.

Where a club is using other premises on a special occasion, there can be no off-supplies at all. Any liquor supplied there is for consumption at the event only, and it is illegal to allow any member to take liquor away from those premises. This does not, of course, apply to club members transporting any unused stock back to the clubhouse for subsequent supply during permitted hours.

11 Food hygiene regulations

Q As a result of a local outbreak of food poisoning we received a visit from the local environmental health officer and although we were not involved he told me that the regulations applied to our bar. I told him we were a private members' club, but he said we were still covered. Is this true?

A Yes, it is. The Food Safety Act 1990 covers almost all catering and food businesses, whether they operate for profit or not. It also covers both food and drink, so it will apply to clubs which have a bar but no actual food preparation.

Under the Food Safety (General Food Hygiene) Regulations 1995, there are requirements for the operators or proprietors of food businesses to ensure that the preparation, storage, handling, offering for sale and service of food is carried out in an hygienic way. In place of the specific rules and prohibitions under previous regulations, the current law set general standards. Schedule 1 of the Regulations gives more detailed requirements for food premises, including equipment, personal hygiene, waste, training of food handlers and others matters. There is also a requirement for anyone working in a food handling area (which includes behind the bar) to report to the operator any illness, wound, infection or other medical condition which might contaminate food. In certain circumstances, the club may have to refuse to allow such a person to work, if it might pose a risk to health.

Your local EHO might well make recommendations about the layout, cleaning and equipment in food rooms in the club, which you would do well to heed. In serious cases he can issue a improvement notice and then close down the club if he feels that it poses an imminent risk to health. This has been done in rare instances.

Although the acquisition of training qualifications is not mandatory, it would be a good idea to consider basic training of food handlers in food hygiene and preparation.

12 Wine by the glass

Q I understand that there are regulations covering the sale of wine by the glass. Will they apply in this club and will we have to have stamped wine glasses, like beer mugs?

A Since January 1995 there has been a legal order fixing the measures in which wine may be sold by the glass. These are 125ml and 175ml. This will apply to all premises in which wine and other alcoholic drinks are sold by retail.

There is no requirement that one of these measures should be chosen and different wines may be served in different sized glasses, as long as they comply with the regulations as to quantity. This normally means wine glasses which are government stamped with a line to show capacity.

There is a further regulation covering wine sold by carafe, usually in restaurants, where the quantity sold must be displayed on the menu or price list, or on the container in which it is presented to the customer. Failure to do this could result in a prosecution.

However, as with all the regulations covering sales of intoxicating liquor by measure, nothing applies to registered members' clubs. As they do not 'sell' the liquor in the legal sense, but merely supply it among themselves, there can be no prosecutions under weights and measures legislation.

13 Passing off in licensed club

Q We have been warned about staff giving a different brand of drink from the one asked for. My question is: is this actually illegal if the customer accepts it, and who would take out the prosecution against us?

A The offence which you describe is known in the trade as 'passing off' and it can in certain circumstances be considered contrary to trading standards legislation. But the more common procedure is for the offended company to take out a civil action against the outlet.

In recent years, companies have appeared to be very sensitive about the substitution of another brand for their own, without any indication to the customer. They claim that as they spend a lot of money on advertising and promotion, it is unfair if a lesser brand gains the benefit.

They also claim that often the substitute brand is of inferior quality or is cheaper for the retailer to buy, thus gaining him extra profit through the deception.

Let us be clear about one thing. Giving a different brand when requested for a trade name constitutes passing off. But deliberately pouring an inferior product into a branded bottle in an attempt to swindle customers is a criminal offence and is rightly considered to be far more serious.

If local trading standards officers receive a complaint about the quality of a drink, they will visit the premises and make a test purchase. They may do this incognito, to see what happens when they place their order, or they may declare who they are and ask to take a sample. In a licensed club they cannot be refused, because they have a legal right to make this demand. The liquor there is sold by retail, and trading standards laws apply.

If on analysis they find that the product served was not the one they requested, or as displayed on the pump or bottle, then they may prosecute either under the Food Act or the Trade Descriptions Act.

If a company suspects that a club is passing off another brand in place of its own, they may also visit incognito to make a test purchase. They will then seek redress in the High Court, through an injunction to prevent the practice and damages for the loss which they have sustained. There have been several successful actions in the recent past.

Bar staff must *always* ask a customer about a substitution before the drink is poured. If the customer then accepts it, no offence is committed.

None of this applies to transactions in a members' club, which is exempt from this part of the law.

14 Change of measures

Q As a special promotion in this club I am thinking of changing the measure for spirits to 35ml instead of 25ml, and advertising 'larger measures at the X Club'. In your opinion would this be legal?

A You do not say in your letter whether you intend to change all your spirit measures in all bars, or only some of them, or in only part of the premises. The legal position is that you would have to make a complete change or none at all. You cannot have different measures in the same premises.

The measuring of spirits is now governed by the Weights and Measures (Intoxicating Liquor) Order 1988. This order stipulates that licensed premises cannot have different measures in different parts of the premises. Gin, rum, vodka and whisky may only be sold in quantities of 25ml or 35ml or multiples of those quantities, and the measure must be the same for all four spirits.

It would not be possible to have your main bars serving these spirits in 25ml measures and the special promotions bar serving in 35ml measures. The reason is that the wording includes the phrase 'quantities...shall be the same for those parts of the premises of which he is the licensee...'

This means that if you hold the licence in respect of the whole club, as I am sure you do, all the bars under that licence must serve the same quantity measure.

15 Portable bar

Q Can you clarify the legal position for us? We have been offered a well-appointed portable bar/caravan for home cricket matches, events etc. Is it legal for us to use this on our sports ground, although it is outside the club premises, and can members and visiting teams use it?

A A certificate of registration is unlike a licence for a pub. It does not rely on a rigid plan of bars, public areas and access. Nor is the supply of liquor limited to one or two specific places in the building. Registration, once granted, allows the club to supply liquor 'on club premises' to members, guests and any persons which the rules of the club allow to be served, subject to section 49 of the Licensing Act 1964.

There is no provision in the Act for the notification to the magistrates of any change in the place or places on the premises where liquor is to be supplied. No prior consent is required from the court for such a change, unless the premises are so altered that they become 'different' premises, for which a variation in the registration certificate would be required.

It seems entirely appropriate, therefore, that the provision of liquor supplies should be made where it is needed, in circumstances which can be controlled by the club. As the supply is to take place on club premises, it is authorised by your existing certificate.

Under your rules, I note that members of visiting sports teams playing bona fide matches against the club may be supplied with intoxicating liquor while visiting the club. This would also apply to the portable bar, if you so desired. Members of the public cannot be supplied with liquor, however, and great care must be exercised to ensure that the facility is not abused and does not lead to sales to casual spectators who are admitted without checking.

16 Bar in other premises

Q This is a registered works club and due to closures a fairly large hall has become available for our use. It is about three miles from the club premises and we would like to know the legal position if we wanted to run an occasional dance or disco there, with a bar. How would we go about

gaining the necessary legal extensions to our certificate?

A If all you intend to do is to use this hall occasionally, then the legal position is that no formal application is required at all. A registered club is entitled, under the licensing laws, to use different premises on special occasions and to supply drinks there, but only to members and guests for consumption at the event.

If, however, you intend to use this hall regularly, there may be an advantage in going to court to have your certificate of registration amended to include it as part of the 'club premises'.

Your current registration certificate allows you to supply liquor to members (and guests) at the registered premises '... or at any premises or place which the club is using on a special occasion for the accommodation of members and to which persons other than members and their guests are not permitted access'.

So, any registered club is allowed to supply drink not only at its own clubhouse, but also on other premises, or in another place (not necessarily a building) as long as entry is restricted to members and their guests.

You, as secretary, are not required to notify the police or the magistrates in advance, nor can they prevent you from making use of this legal concession. The only thing to bear in mind is that the occasion must be 'special' for the club, not a regular Saturday night dance or discotheque.

17 One or the other

Q You have explained that clubs can use other premises on a special occasion without the need to gain an extension or other permission from the magistrates. Does this mean that the club premises must be closed during the hours in question to make the occasion valid?

A You are obviously concerned about the use of the word 'or' in my reply. This might suggest 'either ... or' and mean that if one place was serving drinks, the other would not be able to do so.

That is not my interpretation of this section. In fact, my answer to the previous question stated that a registration certificate allowed a club to supply drinks not only at the club premises but also at another place being used for a special occasion.

The section itself is expressed in negative terms, that is to say, it states that intoxicating liquor shall not be supplied except in these two places. There is no requirement in the section that the premises in respect of which the club is registered should suddenly become 'de-registered' for the period during which the event takes place.

In fact, there are a number of club events which may not involve the membership as a whole. Although it is open to the committee of a members' club to close the whole club or restrict entry to it on the occasion of some special event, it is also permissible to make provision for both participants and non-participants.

Thus, if certain members do not want to attend a special event, they can still be accommodated in the clubhouse while the event takes place. It is not a legal requirement that such a special event should involve the whole membership of the club, to the exclusion of any other activity.

The only restriction placed upon the use of other premises is that only members and their guests may be permitted access. This does not just mean the supply of drink, but physical access to the premises. Visitors and members of the public must be excluded throughout the event in question.

A further, minor point is that no off-supplies may be made at all from the premises used for the special event. Liquor is supplied exclusively for consumption in the premises or place.

18 Liability of licensee

Q As the proprietor of a club, can you tell me whether I am personally responsible for actions taken by my barmaid when I am not present in the building, especially with regard to sales of liquor?

A I assume that you are not only the proprietor of the club, but also the licensee of the premises. This means that you have certain legal obligations which the licensing law makes your responsibility entirely.

When people work for you, they become what are known as your servants or, in some cases, your agents. What they do, they do on your behalf. If they do it badly, or wrongly, or illegally, you may well be responsible in law.

Although the law was changed in 2001 to make bar staff personally responsible for their own actions, the licensing law is still intended to ensure that whoever holds the licence runs his business properly. If someone in your establishment breaks the law in respect of the licence, the law will look to you first of all to find out why you allowed it to happen.

You may well have been absent when the offence took place. But this is not always an excuse. Your responsibility is to ensure that the law is obeyed. Liquor may only be sold by you under the authority of your licence, although you may employ others to make the actual transaction on your behalf. So if an illegal sale is made, you are the person responsible.

19 All-ticket fight

Q On the evening of the World Championship fight, our steward, unknown to us, allowed members to stay on in the club after normal closing time by purchasing raffle tickets for the extra drinks. Afterwards he claimed that no money changed hands and that this was legal. We are very doubtful and would like your ruling and also what we should do about the situation.

A I am aware that there are various 'devices' which people assume can get round the licensing laws. There is also a wide assumption that the rules in this respect are different for private clubs from public houses. They aren't.

The reason for this is that as soon as you receive a certificate of registration for the club bar, you are bound by the terms and conditions of the Licensing Act which apply to all premises serving alcoholic drinks. Permitted hours are laid out in that Act.

This means that unless the club has an extension of some kind, the actual supply of alcoholic drink must stop at the terminal hour. It is not necessary to have a sale to break the law — any form of supply will be considered illegal.

The interesting point here is that because a registered club has no licensee, the privileges of a licensee entertaining his private friends after time do not apply. There is no corresponding concession for the steward or committee of a registered club.

We now turn to your steward's idea of having no money changing hands but using raffle tickets instead. This has no legal validity and is just a device to avoid the suggestion of a sale. Were the police to enter the club after 11.20pm, therefore, they would be entitled to assume that all drinks still on the tables were supplied by the club after the end of permitted hours.

This is important for you as committee members, because it will be you who will be prosecuted in the first instance. The steward may only be charged with 'aiding and abetting' the offence, unless it is very clear to the police that the matter was entirely his doing.

You must take firm action to stop it. This is a case for a formal warning, to demonstrate how serious it is. You realise that actions of this kind could jeopardise the registration certificate entirely.

I am aware that many club people are annoyed that in the past they have not been able obtain extensions for these important sporting events because the magistrates say they are not 'special' for the club. Since the 2002 World Cup decision this may not be such a problem. But that does not mean that you can go ahead and break the law with impunity, or allow someone to do it on your behalf.

Chapter 13
Permitted hours and extensions

1 Notifying hours

Q At our recent committee meeting we decided to extend the bar opening hours at the weekend, particularly in the afternoons. As secretary, do I have to write to the police or the magistrates?

A No, not in this instance. The only notification now required by law is for Christmas Day hours, not the rest of the year, which is now covered by the general licensing hours.

Since the major changes to permitted hours in 1988 and 1995, clubs have enjoyed the same hours as pubs and are not required to fix their hours with the magistrates. The only exception to this is Christmas Day, which still retains an afternoon break under the general law.

Registered clubs can fix their hours on Christmas Day to be different from pubs (always allowing for extensions, anyway). However, there is very limited scope, because there must be a break in the afternoon between three and five, and not more than three and a half hours after five. In practice, this means 12 noon until 3 pm and 7 pm until 10.30 pm, which is exactly the same as pubs.

However, clubs who thought it appropriate could open the bar at 5 pm and close it at 8.30 pm — as long as they had notified the clerk to the magistrates in advance. No notice is required to the police.

In fact, most clubs have fixed their Christmas Day hours simply by stating them in their renewal application during the past ten years.

2 Bar opening hours not in rules

Q The club solicitor tells us that any change in our permitted hours must be approved by the licensing justices and requires a special general meeting of club members. I enclose our rule book and would be grateful for your advice.

A This question highlights what should be in the rules and what should NOT. Opening times are definitely a 'not'. As your rules are currently framed, the permitted hours are written out in some detail. To change them requires a change in the rules themselves, which must be done in accordance with rule 34.

This means a general or special meeting of members, with any motion carried by a majority of at least two thirds of those persons present and entitled to vote.

This is the procedure laid down for any change in the rules of your club, and it must be followed even for the smallest change in bar hours, because they are enshrined in your rule book.

So on this point your solicitor is right. However, my advice to you is to use the general meeting which you must call, NOT to amend the permitted hours in your rules, but to remove this wording entirely and substitute a better rule which will avoid any difficulty in the future.

What you need to do is to delete all references to the actual hours and substitute what is called an 'enabling rule', vesting the power to change the bar hours from time to time in the committee of the club. Then, such hours as you require will be fixed 'under the rules of the club', but not by them.

Many clubs still use the wording 'The permitted hours for the supply of intoxicating liquor on the club premises shall be fixed in accordance with the terms of the Licensing Act 1964 by a resolution of the committee and notified by the secretary to the clerk to the licensing justices; and no resolution fixing the hours shall have effect until such notification has been given'. In fact, only Christmas Day hours now need to be notified (*see previous question*).

To this can be added further wording that the permitted hours will be displayed on the club notice board, or contained in the byelaws of the club, a copy of which is obtainable from the secretary.

Remember that the bar opening times are not necessarily the same as the club opening times — clubs may be open for a number of activities while the bar is closed. Both sets of times should be in the byelaws, not the rules.

3 Earlier start in the morning

Q In February this year all the public houses in our area had their permitted hours changed. This has resulted in our hours now being different from theirs. Do we have to change our hours immediately and what is the procedure?

A It is important for any club which is in an area where there have been recent changes in permitted hours to study their own situation carefully. Limited changes can be made at the Brewster Sessions which take place in February every year, which could affect clubs, but it is rare for clubs to be represented there.

Now that weekday hours are the same for everyone, there is very little scope for change. The only time for the licensing justices to alter hours is now in the early morning, if they think the drinking public requires it.

So where in any licensing district an extra hour or half an hour is added between 10 am and 11 am, clubs will also be entitled to take advantage of this addition, without making a separate application.The change is made by order of the justices, who will normally ensure that it is publicised to all holders of licences in their division, and presumably to all registered clubs as well.

But you must check your rules first. If the permitted hours for the club are contained in them, then they will need to be changed. In practice, a change to an earlier weekday start is automatic for clubs, because they now follow the 'general licensing hours'. So if the permitted hours are not included in the rules, a simple notification to the bar staff and members is quite sufficient.

4 Club hours in Scotland

Q Can you inform us whether the same permitted hours for registered clubs apply in Scotland, and if not, what are the major differences between the ways in which club hours may be fixed in England and Scotland?

A First of all, the registration and conduct of clubs is contained in an entirely different Act of Parliament—the Licensing (Scotland) Act 1976. This set up an entirely new system, particularly with regard to permitted hours and their extensions, which has been relatively successful, with England and Wales only catching up in 1988. However, there are more restricted hours on Sundays.

Briefly, the normal bar hours for clubs in Scotland are from 11 am until 11 pm on weekdays, the same as in England, but on Sundays between 12.30 pm and 2.30 pm and between 6.30 pm and 11 pm. Drinking-up time is 15 minutes instead of ten.

Sporting or athletic clubs which fulfil certain conditions of operation between October and March may apply to the sheriff for considerable alterations to their permitted hours on Sundays, to cater for players.

The hours may be changed to 12.30 until 2 pm and then 4 pm to 9 pm, giving the same duration of six and a half hours, but allowing the bars to open earlier in the evening, where daylight play is required.

In addition, a registered club may apply to the quarterly meeting of the Licensing Board for a regular or occasional extension of permitted hours, to cater for club function 'or a private function organised by an individual member or group of members of the club'.

In the case of a regular order, the police may apply to the licensing board for such hours to be restricted or curtailed 'in the interests of public order or safety'.

5 Secretary entertains

Q I am the secretary of a social club. A licensee friend of mine entertained my wife and I the other night and said that under the licensing laws he was able to buy us drinks after 'time'. Is that the same for me if I entertain my friends in the club?

A I am afraid it is not the same for you, or for your club staff. Different rules apply for licensed premises under the Licensing Act. Drink may not normally be sold or supplied except during the permitted hours, but section 63 of the Act lists certain exceptions to this strict rule. For example, drinks for residents on any premises, the ordering of off-supplies (but not taking away), and the sale of drink to pubs or clubs by wholesalers.

The other exceptions apply only to licensed premises and not to clubs. These are:

● the taking of liquor from the premises by a person residing there;

● supplying drink to private friends of residents, or private friends of a person carrying on or in charge of the business;

● supply by the licensee to his own staff at his own expense.

The secretary of a registered members' club is not the licensee. Neither is the steward. Nobody 'holds' a licence for the club; the secretary may well keep a copy of the registration certificate, but that does not place him in the same position as a licensee of a public house.

When the permitted hours fixed by the club are over, no further supply of liquor may take place unless there has been some form of extension granted to the club. There is no special privilege for any officials of the club.

6 Staff after time

Q This is a small proprietary club, for which I hold the licence. What is the position with regard to drinks for staff after time? We have been visited by the police and I am concerned about the legality of what we do at present.

A The question of staff drinks in a licensed club is specifically covered by the Licensing Act 1964. As long as you comply with the conditions outlined there, you need have no fear of the law.

Outside permitted hours, drinks may be consumed by persons employed in the premises, if the liquor is supplied *at the expense of their employer or the person in charge of the business.*

Staff may not themselves buy drinks outside permitted hours on your premises, nor may they entertain their own friends. The only persons who can do so are residents on the premises, or a manager in charge of the business, or you yourself.

Staff are not permitted to build up a 'credit' by postponing drinks bought for them by club members. Even if the money has already gone into the till, the supply of drinks outside permitted hours is still prohibited by the Act, they would have to wait until the next period of permitted hours in order to take advantage of the hospitality.

None of this answer applies to registered members' clubs. There is no provision in the Licensing Act for club staff and it would be an offence for the secretary or steward to allow consumption after permitted hours. The committee, although technically 'employers', are not covered by this concession, which applies only to licensed premises.

7 Drinks at special events

Q I am confused about temporary bars set up in marquees for e.g. five-a-side football, company cricket matches etc. Am I right in thinking that one does not have to apply for an extension, even for Sunday afternoons?

A It depends where the bar is situated and who uses it. You are right in thinking that registered clubs have a special dispensation when it comes to running temporary bars outside their own premises. Section 39 of the Licensing Act 1964 allows any club which holds a certificate of registration to supply liquor to members and guests 'at any premises or place which the club is using on a special occasion and to which persons other than members and their guests are not permitted access.'

This right is built into the licensing laws and does not require any extra permission from the magistrates or the police. There is not even a legal requirement to notify them in advance.

The advantage of this procedure is that the permitted hours do not apply to the 'other premises' at all. As long as the club complies with the requirements and restricts entry to members and guests, it can operate a bar at any time of the day or

130

night, for the duration of the special event.

But it may be that your sportsground is not considered as separate premises and is already covered by your registration certificate. In this case, although you would not require any additional permission to supply liquor there during normal permitted hours, if you wanted to keep the bar open on Sunday afternoons, then you would require a special order of exemption from the local magistrates.

So the answer depends entirely on whether the sportsground is considered part of the registered club premises or not. If it is distinct and separate from the club building, or on a different site, or different part of the overall company area, then my view is that you can take advantage of section 39. But if it is integral with the existing registered club, then you will have to seek an extension.

8 All-night event

Q We are holding a marathon games event to raise money for charity. The bar will close as normal at 11 pm but those participating will be allowed to bring in bottles and cans of their own for private consumption during the night. No sales will be made. Do we need an extension from the magistrates for this? Previously, they told us that an extension was not required for a brewery promotion when beer was given away to those attending.

A This letter poses a problem. There would seem to be a mistaken view prevailing that the law is not involved if liquor is given away or consumed by individuals without supply by the club.

I am afraid this simply is not the case. Both the supply and consumption of liquor outside permitted hours can be illegal, whatever the circumstances.

It makes no difference that these are registered club premises. In this respect the law is exactly the same as it is for public houses. The permitted hours are laid down by law for both types of premises, and consumption outside those hours, unless it is authorised in some way, contravenes the licensing laws.

Let us take the brewery promotion first. It is true that the club is not supplying the beer, and it is a private function to which persons other than members and guests are invited. The magistrates appear to have taken the view that because no sale is involved, then there is no need for an extension. But there is no sale involved when your club supplies intoxicating liquor to members and guests, yet you still require both an authority to make that supply and an extension if you intend to do it outside normal permitted hours.

Section 59 of the Licensing Act 1964 states that '**no person** shall, except during the permitted hours ... **supply** to any person in ... premises in respect of which a club is registered, any intoxicating liquor...'

This is a general prohibition. Note that it does not specify who does the supplying or who is supplied: it is the act of supply of liquor which is prohibited.

So this special promotional event outside permitted hours would require an extension to comply strictly with the law.

Turning to your marathon, apart from the fact that the event would probably qualify for an extension in its own right, there is a second important prohibition in the same section of the Act.

This states that, except during the permitted hours 'no person shall consume in such premises **any intoxicating liquor**.'

Again, that is a general prohibition and does not mention who supplied the drink in question. The object of the section is to prevent consumption of liquor on registered or licensed premises outside the permitted hours. So my view is that both events would require an extension or even an occasional permission to allow for the activities which you have described.

9 Extension guidelines

Q Our local bench seem to have a fixed list when it comes to extensions. Certain celebrations are allowed, but others are not. We find it very difficult to understand their reasons. Can you say whether there is anything we can do about their rigid rules?

A It is true that the majority of benches are trying to achieve greater consistency in the grant of applications by following guidelines produced by the Justices' Clerks' Society and producing a list of what will be considered 'special' or not.

Of course, the guidelines will not necessarily distinguish between members' clubs and licensed premises such as pubs and this is where some clubs feel they are missing out. It is important that magistrates realise that in every case:

● the application must be dealt with on its merits; and

● the magistrates have a discretion which must be exercised judicially, not on pre-formed prejudice.

The *Good Practice Guide* from the Justices' Clerks' Society lists the occasions that will normally be regarded as 'special' for special order of exemption purposes. The list includes:

Silver, Ruby, Gold or Diamond Wedding Anniversaries;

18th and 21st Birthdays; 40th, 50th, 60th, 70th and every ten years thereafter;

Christening, Wedding and Engagement parties;

Annual dinners or dances of genuine local or national organisations;

Christmas and New Year; and 25th and 50th Anniversaries of significant events.

The 'grey areas' include:—

Festivals, sporting events or tournaments; going away, homecoming or retirement parties; beginning or end of term dances; conferences; draws and raffles; and 'games nights'.

The problem of course is that if your forthcoming event is on the 'grey' list you will be annoyed if it is turned down and will complain about inconsistency. If it is one of the obvious special occasions, you will accept the extension without comment.

Although both pubs and clubs apply for the same set of extensions, it may be that certain special club events would be accepted, whereas a similar pub event would not. While you have local discretion you will always have inconsistency of decisions.

10 London extensions

Q I am the secretary of a social club in the East End of London. I am new to the job I would be grateful for guidance on how we can obtain an extension for Jubilee procession day in this area. Many of our members are taking part and will want to use the club both before and after the event.

A As your club is situated in the London area, different rules apply to you for the application and grant of a special order of exemption. Outside the Metropolitan Police area, or the City of London, such applications are dealt with by the local magistrates' court.

For clubs within the Metropolitan Police area, the function of the justices is taken over by the Commissioner, so that applications for this type of extension are made to the police and not to the magistrates' clerk. The procedure is not given in the Licensing Act, but New Scotland Yard has its own licensing department which deals with extensions of this kind, and has established a procedure for handling requests for extensions. Normally, you should make written application at least one month in advance of the event for which you need an extension.

The easiest method for you is to visit your local police station, where you will be informed of the procedure. Often, applications of this type can be dealt with almost entirely locally, but my advice is to start early, as the police prefer a reasonable period of notice.

Unlike the magistrates, who are in a position to grant a special order of exemption 'on the spot' at a court hearing, the police do not have an open court in which this can be done. So the vast majority of applications are dealt with entirely in writing.

You will be asked to complete a form of application, giving the name and address of the club, the date for which application is made and the additional hours required for the extension. Obviously, you will not need an extension for the actual day of the Golden Jubilee, which is already covered by a special government Order until 1 am.

The majority of extensions of this type which are applied for in the London area are granted, after due enquiries have been made. But it is not always the case that the hours requested will be granted in entirety. The licensing department, or the local police, might feel that the hours claimed are too long or too late. In such cases they will not throw out the application but may authorise a more limited extension.

11 Special hours for New Year

Q What is the position on New Years Eve? Will clubs still have to apply to the magistrates for extensions as usual?

A Not if the Government's new plan goes ahead. It is likely that from 2002 onward, New Year's Eve will have a special automatic extension for all clubs and licensed premises.

The Special Occasions Licensing Order is likely to allow continuous opening throughout the night of 31 December until the normal start of permitted hours on 1 January. Clubs and pubs may therefore continue to serve as long as they like on that day.

In practice, very few establishments have stayed open throughout the whole period, because the demand from customers or members was not there. After all, there is no point wasting money by paying bar staff to sit up all night if the members have gone home!

The extension will be of blanket operation, so that all clubs will be able to take advantage of it without making any form of application or notifying the police. Similarly, there is no need to specify how late you are going to stay open — the decision on shutting the bar is entirely yours.

Although the normal protection of registered clubs from police entry will apply, special care should be taken to ensure that there are not incidents of drunkenness or rowdy behaviour associated with the celebration, which might cause the police to take further action. For proprietary clubs, the rights of police and the obligations of the holder of the licence and his staff continue throughout the night.

12 Need to apply for Christmas extensions

Q I have taken over as secretary during the past year and have been asked to apply for extensions for the bar over the Christmas and New Year periods. Local pubs are reported to have obtained theirs, but what do we have to do, or can we just open the same times?

A There appears to be an assumption among club officials that this type of extension is automatic and there is nothing needed to be done. Some blame for this may be attached to the courts and the rest of the licensed trade, who in some cases appear to 'fix' what hours should be allowed several months in advance.

I must point out that, with the exception of New Year's Eve (*see previous question*), each club has to apply to the magistrates on its own behalf for any special order of exemption required for the Christmas period. Failure to do this means that the club must adhere to its own normal permitted hours over the whole period, including Christmas Day.

Because such extensions are becoming commonplace, in line with the *Good Practice Guide* the courts have made it known in advance what dates and times they will consider in respect of what might be termed 'normal' extensions for the period, that is, to premises without any special function arranged.

If, however, your club has one or two events on special days over the festive season, then you are at liberty to approach the bench with an application for extensions to cover these times as well.

It may be that they will not grant all the extended hours which you require. But you must make some form of application in order to obtain even the minimum extra periods which they are prepared to grant.

My advice is to make application as soon as possible and to contact your local magistrates' clerk who will be able to tell you what procedure the bench has adopted for hearing this type of application.

13 Applying for permissions

Q We recently applied for an occasional permission for an event to which we wanted to invite the public, but the application never got to court. The clerk's office told us we were too late. It was well in advance of the event. What is the legal situation and can the clerk rather than the magistrates make such a ruling?

A First of all, the clerk can certainly make a ruling on the question of proper notice. He cannot place before the licensing justices an application which does not fulfil the requirements of the law, and checking on notices is usually entirely his affair.

The problem is that, unlike all other applications made by registered clubs in respect of liquor, occasional permissions are dealt with by the licensing justices, not the magistrates' court.

While magistrates will sit regularly throughout the year, the licensing justices only meet a maximum of monthly, and in many cases less often than that. There is also a requirement that notice of the application must be given to the clerk to the justices 'not less than 21 days' before the date of the event, and that if notice is received fifteen days or less before the next licensing sessions, it will have to be held over until the next sessions, which may well be too late.

So you really need to count, and to work out the sessions prior to the event, to be sure of being heard. Phone the licensing office to get the dates of the next few sessions, and write them down. Then make sure that there is a sessions at least seven days prior to the event, to be on the safe side and count 15 days back from that. To be entirely safe, make your application at least **one month** before the sessions you want to use.

14 Club events only

Q We currently have no ruling allowing visitors to the club to buy drinks, so to get round this for certain hirings we applied for occasional permissions. The clerk has now informed us that the applications are invalid, as the events are not being run by the club (even though we are supplying the drink). What can we do about this?

A An occasional permission does not take the place of a normal club extension for a special event, to extend the permitted hours. It is specifically intended for those occasions when the public are to be admitted to the club for a club function.

A number of clubs make their premises available for hire by members or even by outside organisations. There is nothing illegal in this, as long as the basic nature of the club remains unchanged. Clearly, if a club turns into a hiring 'business' then it ceases to be a genuine members' club and its registration is in jeopardy. But occasional hirings are not entirely prohibited under the present law.

If the rules of the club so provide, the persons attending the event may be admitted as visitors, and the club may supply them with intoxicating liquor simply under the authority of the registration certificate. This is clearly preferable to an occasional licence or occasional permission.

When the club has no such rule, or it has been vetoed by the magistrates, then an occasional permission will not take its place. This authority will not allow the club to cater for events which are, in essence, unconnected with its own affairs.

If the hiring of the premises is undertaken by any bona fide organisation, then an officer or another individual authorised by the organisation may apply on behalf of the hirers. But if it is merely an individual hiring, or a wedding party or similar family event, an occasional permission is not appropriate and can justifiably be refused under the provisions of section 1 of the Licensing (Occasional Permissions) Act 1983.

15 How many permissions?

Q We have had great success with club open days to which non-members are invited. I have heard that you can only obtain four occasional permissions a year, but we might want to do more than this next year. Is there any way round it?

A In 1997, the number of occasional permissions which can be granted to eligible organisations or branches in a twelve month period was raised from 4 to 12.

Although this appears to 'come into line' with the *Little Ship Club* ruling, it does no such thing, and the rules on special occasions should not be confused with this. Occasional permissions are an entirely separate application, and in fact have nothing to do with club registration, because unregistered clubs and societies can apply for them too.

As far as assessing how many permissions have been granted, there are different practices by committees regarding the period to which the limitation on the number of occasional permissions applies. The limit of 12 occasional permissions relates to any period of twelve months in respect of functions held by the same organisation or branch and is not confined to a calendar year. This means that it is now a requirement for applicants for occasional permissions to state on their form of application details of any previous permissions granted within the twelve month period prior to the date of the application.

When the limit was four, some clubs tried to get round the limit by making application on behalf of a 'branch' or 'section'. With the new increased limit, this is not such an urgent problem.

16 Extension food

Q We understand that we can apply for a one hour extension in the evening on a regular basis, if we supply food. A local clubman has said that all we need are sandwiches and rolls for people staying on. Another club I know gives people a meal ticket with the price of admission. We have regular entertainment. Is this sufficient?

A There is far more to the operation of a supper hour certificate than would be suggested by the comments made by your acquaintances. A plate of sandwiches is by no means sufficient. The grant of this extension requires the magistrates to be satisfied, in the case of a club:

● that the premises are suitable for the provision of substantial refreshment.
● that they are habitually used for this purpose.
● that intoxicating liquor will only be supplied to persons taking table meals in the premises.
● that the supply will take place in a part usually set aside for meals, and for consumption by members as an ancillary to their meals.

This means that on the application, you must satisfy the court that part of the club where the entertainment is provided is set aside for persons to eat, and is not just the normal bar of the premises. You must also show adequate catering facilities, including a fully equipped kitchen and probably a menu, and evidence that meals are regularly provided.

You cannot approach the court with a promise to provide sandwiches and rolls and expect them to grant this type of extension. They will not accept that as fulfilling the conditions.

The sandwich 'myth' may have grown up as a result of certain premises failing to continue their operations under the same conditions as when the certificate was granted. For example, they close the kitchens, they change the tables or bar area, and gradually the premises lose the essential catering aspect.

It is then that plates of sandwiches are introduced in an attempt to comply with what is seen as 'the food rule'.

The issuing of a meal ticket is meaningless unless food is actually provided to all persons using the premises. It is not the same as a special hours certificate, the late-night extension where everyone is **not** required to have a meal. A supper hour certificate relies on a restaurant service of some kind for everyone present.

I think you must discuss the implications of this with your management before you embark on any application to the courts.

17 Late Saturdays

Q Is there any way we as a workingmen's club can open late on Saturday evenings on a regular basis? We usually have entertainment and would like to go on until midnight, rather than close the bar at 11 pm

A The time you require is outside the normal permitted hours for your district, so that you cannot merely change your rules. You must obtain a regular extension from the magistrates.

A special order of exemption is unlikely to be granted, because every Saturday night would not be considered 'special'. So that leaves one or other of the regular extensions available to both clubs and licensed premises.

The problem is that a supper hour certificate can only operate in a part of the premises specifically set aside for table meals. Every member staying on would therefore have to be supplied with a meal. Drinks could not be supplied from the normal bars, but if the club has a restaurant or self-service area, this could qualify.

The more satisfactory solution is a special hours certificate for Saturdays only, limited to midnight. Such a certificate can be granted for one night of the week, provided there is regular live entertainment and substantial refreshment available for members. You will have to produce evidence of this in court, on your application to the magistrates.

The certificate can last up to 2 am where required. The magistrates may impose an earlier closing time, on application by the police.

This certificate does not require everyone to sit down and have a meal, but substantial refreshments must be available in sufficient quantity for those who attend. There must also be music and dancing during the whole period for which the extension is sought, or entertainment of a similar kind (a cabaret show would qualify under this rule).

18 Special hours, special terms

Q I have a special hours certificate which runs for two nights a week, on Fridays and Saturdays. Can I extend this to cover Thursday and Sunday as well?

A Yes, you can, but before doing so you must be sure that the extension of hours is going to be used by your members. You cannot apply for such a variation unless you intend to operate regularly on those evenings.

Under section 78A of the Licensing Act 1964 there is provision for the licensing justices to vary a special hours certificate to cover other days of the week in addition to those for which it was originally granted. However, the application procedure is more or less identical to an application for grant of the certificate in the first place.

You may also need to vary your public entertainment licence (PEL) so as to cover late opening on Thursdays and Sundays. This is best done before you make application to the justices.

Although operation on Sunday evenings has now been allowed, following a deregulation order in 2001, the hours of operation are normally limited to 12.30 am. Prior to most bank holidays, this is extended to 2 am. In some areas there have been minor problems over Sunday evenings, and it might be advisable to place the application in the hands of an experienced licensing solicitor.

I have noted that in certain areas of the country the police are checking up on the operation of these late-night certificates and are seeking to use their powers to request revocation under section 81 of the Act, on the grounds that the premises are not being used as mentioned in section 77 of the Act.

The police will also seek revocation because they find that persons are resorting to the premises for the purpose of obtaining intoxicating liquor, rather than partaking of food, or dancing.

If the justices do revoke the certificate, you may not re-apply for at least two months from the date of revocation, and the justices may extend this 'ban' for up to one year, if they see fit, so it can be quite a serious matter.

There are, of course, other powers which affect the operation of special hours certificates, the main one being the power to limit or curtail the terminal hour to a time earlier than 2 am (3 am in London). This power is being used more, on the grounds that the use of the premises causes annoyance or disturbance to neighbours. Again, the limitation can be challenged after a period of time and cannot be imposed as a permanent ban if there is no further disturbance in the vicinity.

19 Free meal tickets

Q In order to encourage more youngsters to use our disco on the slack nights Monday and Tuesday, we have started issuing a number of free meal tickets for use after 11.00 pm when our extension starts. A colleague has told me that this is against the law, and they must pay for food. What is your view?

A You do not tell me what type of extension you have on these nights. There are two which spring to mind, but the circumstances for each are different. First of all, there is nothing illegal in giving out free meal tickets as an incentive. But you must ensure that any promotional material does not contravene the Trade Descriptions Act or other consumer legislation (i.e. if there is a limitation on members, it should be stated, or the days of operation).

Secondly, do not assume that the giving of unredeemed meal tickets qualifies a certain area of the premises for a supper hour extension. This is not the case. Under this type of extension, persons attending must actually take a table meal and the place you are using must be set aside for this purpose. This means that if persons are merely drinking, but are in possession of a free meal ticket, the law is still being broken.

The situation with a special hours certificate is different. The club qualifies for this extension by persuading the justices that music, dancing 'and substantial refreshment' are available during the whole of the additional hours when drink can be supplied.

So there must be food readily available for anyone who wishes to have it. Again, the mere issuing of a meal ticket, with no food either in preparation or visible to those attending, can be used by the police as evidence that the terms of the extension are being broken.

20 Only those attending

Q I understand that a recent ruling has stated that only those actually participating in an event may make use of an extension. We have two bars in this club. Does the extension only apply to one of them?

A I am not aware of any recent decision which has amended the legal situation with regard to extensions. But it has been customary for some time for magistrates to require an undertaking from applicants with regard to the conduct of the extension.

A special order of exemption is granted to extend the permitted hours on the occasion of some special event in the club. Its effect is to change the permitted hours in the premises as a whole, so that the sale or supply of drink would not be illegal anywhere.

This means that if the magistrates make no stipulation, or the matter is not raised, the whole club receives the benefit of the extension. It is then up to the committee to decide whether other bars should remain open, or whether the extra time will be limited to the room or hall in which the event is taking place.

If the court does ask for the supply of drinks to be limited, it would be sensible to comply. Although they do not have power to demand it, the discovery that an undertaking had been broken would make them far less amenable to future applications.

21 Extra for shift workers

Q Is there any way in which we can extend our permitted hours by half an hour during the week? We have a large number of shift workers who come off duty just as the bar is closing, and they would like a drink before going home.

A If you are already using the permitted hours for the locality to their fullest extent, you cannot make a change on your own behalf. If you are seeking a time beyond 3 pm in the afternoon, or 11 pm at night, then you will need a special extension.

It seems to me that you have a very good case for what is known as a General Order of Exemption under section 74 of the Licensing Act 1964. The premises are situated on the site and the club is not used except by employees of the company. If, as you say, there is a considerable demand for bar facilities after a shift has ended, then you may succeed in this application.

Clubs which are situated in the immediate vicinity of a place 'where people follow a trade or calling' are entitled to an indefinite extension of this type, granted by the local magistrates after examining all the circumstances. Works clubs have succeeded before in obtaining such an order, and you should prepare your case at once for submission to the magistrates.

What you need is clear evidence among the workforce of a need for additional bar hours for those who have finished work at unusual times of the day or night, plus union or other representatives to support the application to the magistrates.

22 Drinking up on extensions

Q I am a club steward and would like to know why we cannot have drinking up time on the end of extensions like pubs do. It means that we have to call 'time' at 11.58 and have everyone out by midnight, which is impossible.

A I should be very interested to know who gave you this information on extensions. It is completely inaccurate! Clubs are in exactly the same position as pubs in this respect.

To take your example, where the local pubs have applied for bank holiday extensions to the magistrates, clubs are entitled to seek the same hours. So it may be that you were granted an Easter extension up until 12 midnight, adding an extra hour to the normal permitted hours in the club.

But an extension **adds** to the permitted hours. This means that section 63 of the Licensing Act 1964 operates at midnight as it would normally do at 11 pm. It states that consumption may continue for a period of 20 minutes 'after the end of any period forming part of those hours.' This means that drinking up time after your extension lasts from midnight until 12.20 am.

I think you are referring to the club rules, which state the opening and closing times of the club premises. It is true that these do give a closing time of midnight on weekdays and stipulate that members should have left the premises by then.

The reason for this rule is to allow for the club premises to be locked up by the steward or other employee and is a common one for social clubs, who wish to advise members when they are permitted access to the club. It is not a requirement that these times should comply with normal 'pub times', as some people think.

So the situation is that the club does have a drinking-up time on these extensions, but it will conflict with the current club rules. The answer is to get this rule changed (or removed to the byelaws, where it can be properly adapted to suit the club's needs). Alternatively, on the occasion of the extension the committee may post a notice stating that the club will be closed at 12.30 on the evening in question.

23 Late hours change

Q We have a rather special situation here, in that we have an exemption until 1 am for our staff club. Recently we have decided that we should close at midnight, because of lack of demand, but only Sundays to Thursdays. Who do we have to notify about this, and will we lose the extension entirely?

A What you hold is obviously a general order of exemption, granted by the magistrates because the members of your club work 'unsocial hours', often throughout the night. The special feature of this general order is that it is more or less permanent. It does not require renewal and lasts until it is given up or cancelled by the magistrates — usually on application by the police.

For pubs and other licensed premises, it has come to be known as the 'market day extension', but it is quite appropriate to clubs, particularly staff clubs, where drinks may be required outside the normal permitted hours.

Your general order appears to cover the full seven day period—which is quite understandable when your staff are working late every night of the week. However, there is no need for you to make a formal approach to anyone in these circumstances. You should just close the bar earlier than the exemption order permits.

What may eventually happen is that the police will apply to the magistrates for cancellation of the order, because there is no need for it in its present form. Before that happens, you may decide that you only need a midnight closing anyway. But it may not happen at all, because there are obviously certain nights of the week when the extension is used to its fullest extent.

So my view is that it would be best to go ahead with your plan and wait for someone else to raise the issue. You could then claim that this was a temporary measure, due to unusual circumstances, and that it was still a necessary extension for your workers. I do not think, however, that any objection will be raised at this stage to what you plan.

24 Changes over Easter

Q This is a proprietary discotheque which I have recently taken over. I hear that Easter permitted hours are sometimes different and should like to know how it affects us.

A Prior to 1985, the operation of both extended hours orders and special hours certificates had been prohibited on Good Friday and curtailed on two other days, much to the annoyance of club and entertainment venue owners.

The situation is now that although normal permitted hours on Good Friday are Sunday hours, either of these two extensions will operate to its full extent on that day, subject to any limitation still imposed by the local authority on the entertainment licence for that day.

So if the entertainment licence is limited on Good Friday, then the permitted hours will last just until midnight. If, as in rare cases, the PEL does not operate on Good Friday, there will be no extra time at all.

On Easter Sunday, although it is a Bank Holiday weekend, the special hours certificate will only operate until 12.30 am instead of 2 am (which applies on other bank holiday Sundays).

So there are special limits on your operation which you should check with the local licensing office to ensure that you are complying with the law.

Chapter 14
Betting and gaming

1 Gaming registration

Q We are a members' club and someone has told me that if we have any gaming on the premises we must be registered under the Gaming Act. We hold a ten-year certificate of registration from the magistrates for the club. Is this sufficient?

A There are two types of registration under the Gaming Act 1968 which are entirely different from the registration you already hold for the club. This means that unless you intend to involve the club in certain restricted games such as pontoon or chemin-de-fer, played in accordance with the Gaming Act (Registration under Part II) Regulations 1969, it is not worth considering registration under this part of the Act.

The only advantage is to enable clubs whose members wish to indulge in equal chance gaming such as poker to make a charge for play in excess of 60p, the maximum permitted under section 40 of the Gaming Act. Bridge and whist clubs, however, are entitled to make a charge of up to £15 per day for participation in those games alone, without requiring registration under Part II.

Bingo, which is the most popular game in members' clubs, may be played as equal chance gaming without the need for registration under Part II. Those bingo clubs which are licensed under Part II are commercial ones, and there is a special procedure for them, as opposed to casinos.

Application is made to the local licensing authority, the justices, at any time of the year. Renewal, as with registration for liquor, lasts for a year and then any period up to ten years as the justices may specify.

Most clubs manage to keep their gaming within the Act's limits, or only run casino-type gaming as incidental to an entertainment on special occasions (*see question 18 in this chapter*). This means that they confine their registration to Part III registration for gaming machines, which is entirely different and involves far less scrutiny and control. Details of both types of registration can be found in the checklist in Appendix A.

Where the club intends to hold lotteries in which tickets are sold to members of the public as well as club members, then a form of registration with the local authority is required. This is dealt with more fully in question 13.

2 Strict rules on betting

Q I have recently read of a series of charges concerning horse race bets against a members' club and would like you to explain the laws relating to betting on club premises.

A The principal offence contained in section 1 of the Betting, Gaming and Lotteries Act 1963 is to 'use, cause or knowingly permit any premises to be used as a place where persons resorting thereto may effect pool betting transactions'.

There is a second offence of 'knowingly permitting any person to use the premises' for making 'any other betting transactions' with persons resorting to the premises.

Section 1 is only concerned with places which are not licensed for betting under the Act. There is no specific reference to clubs or other places licensed for the sale of liquor, although clearly registered clubs are caught by the general prohibition of the section, because they are not licensed for betting at all.

The word 'betting' as used by you may have several meanings. In the case of the committee, you mean 'allowing betting transactions in the club'. In the case of the members, you mean 'making betting transactions with someone who is acting as a bookmaker'.

In certain cases, it has been held that a club member or employee himself has been the person with whom the betting transactions are made. This is a serious offence and can result not only in a prosecution and heavy fine but also in the possible loss of the club registration.

The second type of offence which a club official can commit is 'knowingly permitting' the club to be used by a bookmaker or bookmaker's representative as a place where bets may be placed, or where winnings are paid out. Because the evidence required by the court is of 'use' of the premises, it is likely that the police will keep watch to ensure that there have been a number of examples of betting transactions taking place on the premises. If they decide to prosecute the club, it will be either because the committee has connived at the offence or has deliberately turned a blind eye to what is clearly going on in the premises.

The only elements of betting allowed on club premises are the writing out of personal betting slips for subsequent visits to the licensed betting office, the transfer of a completed slip to a personal friend for taking to the licensed betting office, or the telephoning on an open telephone line of account bets to a bookmaker.

3 Bingo duty not charged

Q We run very successful bingo nights in our club, but I recently saw a letter from Customs and Excise about paying bingo duty. Do we have to pay this if we are a members' club?

A Bingo duty for members' clubs was fortunately ended in 1992, when the Finance Act introduced an exemption. Formerly, there were minimum thresholds, which still exist for commercial bingo but which do not apply in the case of clubs and societies.

Bingo duty, according to schedule 3 of the Betting and Gaming Duties Act 1981, as amended, will not be charged if a person's eligibility to participate in that bingo depends upon his being a member of a particular society or his being a guest of such a member or of the society.

Obviously, commercial bingo clubs which are licensed under Part II of the Gaming Act will continue to pay bingo duty, as will other organisations where the total prize money in any one day is over £500 and in any one week above £1500. But that will not apply to the type of bingo you play in your club, however large the prize on offer.

4 Snowball ban

Q We run weekly bingo sessions at this club, limited to members and their own guests. Currently we run a 'snowball' from some of the stake money. Is this allowed and if not, would we be allowed to make a small charge, say 25p, for club funds?

A You may indeed make a charge for participating, in addition to the charge which you make for the cards. The maximum permissible in your case is in fact 60p, so your suggestion can be implemented immediately. Such a charge may go straight to club funds.

The charge may also be devoted to the expenses of running the bingo, because all the stakes must be returned as prizes. You are not allowed to make any deductions for expenses from that money, or to keep any of it for club funds.

As the chances in the gaming must be equally favourable to all the players, I am afraid that 'snowballs' of this type are not permitted. Stake money hazarded by one group of people is retained by the club for possible winnings by another group. The chances thereby become unequal, in that a person in the second group is able to win previously-staked money. This type of rollover is not allowed for club bingo.

The answer is to create a special prize, perhaps from the added income from the entrance charge, which may be added on until won. This would mean that the prize would not be derived from previously staked money, and would therefore be legal.

Bingo may also be played as an entertainment under section 41 of the Gaming Act 1968, in which case some of the stake money may be retained by the club. But if you wish to promote the gaming principally for the benefit of members, or have relatively high stakes and prizes, the first way is preferable.

5 Ban on guests

Q In our club there is a rule for bingo that guests may not win the snowball. This seems to be unfair when they have paid for their cards. Is the club allowed to make this rule and stop the payout?

A You do not enclose any rules for the playing of bingo in your club. It may be that these 'rules' are not written down, but are just accepted by those participating.

Although it is up to clubs to make rules governing the conduct of gaming and other activities on their premises, these must not be such as to break the law. It is illegal to prevent a participant in gaming from obtaining an equal chance of winning with all the other players.

It would therefore be in order to make a rule prohibiting guests from playing bingo. But it is not legal to allow them to play and then to stop them winning.

I assume that the snowball occurs in a special game played during the course of the evening, perhaps on a special ticket which is part of a book, for which the participants pay an inclusive price. If this is the case, then there is no way of separating out books for members and for guests. You must either let everyone have the same chance of winning, or stop guests from playing bingo at all.

If you announce at the commencement of the bingo that guests may not participate in the gaming, then any who do may legally be stopped from claiming a prize. But you cannot take their stake money and then announce that they will not be allowed to claim one of the prizes.

6 Late bingo call

Q Can you clear up a point on bingo for us. We call numbers twice, e.g. '2 and 1, twenty-one'. The caller had begun the first part of this call when a member called 'house' on the previous number. The argument was that until the number had been repeated, the previous number still stood. What is your view?

A The technicalities of bingo are a matter for special rules or conditions of play, which should be known to all participants. If it is a house rule in your club that the last number called must be on the card, then it is up to the participants to call *before* the next number is announced.

This, of course, places on the club the obligation to ensure that reasonable time is given for a call to be made, and that they can be heard or seen by the caller at the correct time. In some clubs, where two rooms are being used for bingo, there must be adequate methods of transmitting a call of 'house' to the bingo caller.

If this procedure is followed in your club, it is clear that the call of 'house' was not made at the correct time. Once the next number has been indicated, the last number is, as you say, dead. But great care must be taken to give players the opportunity to beat this deadline.

I do not think that the repetition of the next number makes any difference. If persons had already heard the next number and marked it on their cards, then it could have created a winning line. To allow the late call in those circumstances would deprive that winner of his or her prize, which would be unfair under your rules for bingo.

7 Bingo call not heard

Q The other evening we were participating in a bingo session when I called house, but the caller carried on with another number. People around heard me call out, but a club official stated that as the call was not heard, my chance was lost. What is the legal position?

A The responsibility for being heard rests entirely with the individual player. If they are not heard by the caller and another number is called, then the 'winning' card will not contain the last number called out, which may well contravene the rules of bingo as normally played.

It is not sufficient that those other players around you heard the call. The essential person is the caller who stops the game. If you do not communicate with him, then you lose your chance.

Bingo should not be played in circumstances where all the players cannot be heard or seen by the caller, or his assistant. There is a responsibility on the club to ensure that any call made anywhere in the room or rooms where bingo is being played will be audible on the stage or wherever the calling takes place.

8 Double house call

Q We had a difficult situation at our regular bingo session recently, on which I would like your advice. We use two colours of books for pre-session 'quickies' and two people called 'house' on different coloured tickets, which both had the same numbers. One of the members said it was illegal, and others said that both players should receive the stated prize. We shared the prize money but would welcome your guidance.

A There appears to be nothing actually illegal in what happened in your club. The same thing has been known to happen when only one set of cards is being used, although the fact that you were using two sets obviously increases the risk.

The Gaming Board advises clubs for this reason not to use double sets of tickets for the same game, to minimise the risk of duplication.

My only slight doubt concerns whether, with a duplicate ticket, the chances in the game can be said to be 'equally favourable' to all the players. The two players with duplicate tickets will not be able to win the whole prize, only half of it, while all the other players have a chance of winning the total amount.

But the club cannot really be faulted, unless they were negligent over a long period in this matter. It is clear you had no way of knowing about the duplication, and the chances are that the duplicate tickets would not be winners.

You do not make it clear whether the two colours referred to the two separate games, e.g. blue for the first and green for the second. Obviously, a green ticket cannot be used in the first game, and vice versa. If, however, you merely mixed the tickets for the same game, the two winners must share the prize allocated.

There is no legal requirement that each should receive the full house prize for that game. The prize money available is shared.

9 Free cards for new members

Q Is it legal for us to give a free first game bingo card to all new members on their first visit to the club, as an incentive to continue coming?

A You do not tell me under what conditions bingo is played in your club, but I shall assume that it is either played as an entertainment under section 41 of the Gaming Act 1968, or simply as equal-chance gaming under Part I of the Act.

In the case of section 41 bingo, of course, only one payment may be made for all games played (and that payment may not exceed £4.00). It is clear that persons are allowed to have more than one card or book of cards without affecting the 'equal chance' rule, because they pay a second charge for the second card.

The problem is that where one person has paid for a card and another has not, the chances in the game may not be considered equal because one person is not at risk of losing any money, whereas the other person is. But the actual chances in the game itself are equal between the players, in that each has an equal chance of winning the prize on offer.

If your games are played under the terms of Part I of the Gaming Act, all stake

money must be returned as prizes, and t⸍
participation in the gaming. It migh⸍
record of free cards given by the
matched the *total* number of cards
are supplied at the expense of the c⸍
then complied with.

10 Sign on the line

Q We are a works sports and social ⸍
lottery among the club members. C⸍
members to sign the enclosed docume⸍

A A private lottery in which the sale of tic⸍
members only may be run on different lines f⸍

The rules for such lotteries contained in the Lotteries
allow for a flexibility in their administration. No memb⸍
relative may participate, unless they are also a member of t⸍

I note from the papers enclosed that you are conducting t⸍
regular deductions from salaries. This is perfectly in order, ⸍
concerned signs at this stage and at any time that any amendr⸍
amounts paid. This is a legal requirement when deductions are ⸍
under current legislation.

There is no limit on the amount which may be staked, and pe⸍
more than one chance each in the lottery, as long as the price of each
same.

Again, there are no tickets needed for this lottery. The signatu⸍
application form is enough to 'register' the chance with the promoter. ⸍
participants should be held at all times, together with a list detailing contribu⸍

The most important statement made here is that no person will be allow⸍
participate in the lottery unless they have paid all contributions up to date. As t⸍
contributions are made by means of salary deductions, those who enter the lottery
the beginning will be covered. Provision should be made for persons enterin⸍
during the lottery to catch up on back payments.

You should also note that as this lottery is for club funds, only club members
may participate. If the membership of the club is voluntary, employees who are not
club members are not entitled to enter. People who all work on the same premises
may run a lottery, but in such a case all the money must be returned as prizes.

11 Free snowball

Q We are considering running a snowball draw to attract more members
to use the club. It is based on the production of membership cards,
which are all numbered. If the member in question is not present when
the draw is made, then the money is carried forward until next week. Is this
legally possible?

A I can see no objection to this scheme at all. As a private members' club, you
are entitled to run free lotteries of this type as often as you wish.

w, the problem with snowball prizes is that they often break the
of gaming, because the persons who contributed to the earlier
ve a chance of winning the subsequent games.
whole membership list is used for a free lottery of this type, every
equal chance of winning, and in addition has risked no money.
till classed as gaming, because the Gaming Act defines it as 'the
me of chance for money or money's worth, whether any person
ne is at risk of losing any money or money's worth or not'.
at a member may not be present in the club when his number is called
ct the fairness of the draw. He or she has the opportunity to be there
rize, and the conditions of the draw make it clear that personal
with membership card is a necessary requirement. If the person is not
the time the draw is announced, then they forfeit the prize and it is
er until the next week.
is no requirement that special tickets have to be printed for such a club
u may use any device for selecting the membership number, as long as it
all the members.

Unclaimed tote tickets

Q During the months prior to Christmas we had three unclaimed
winning tickets in our tote, which is run for the club benevolent fund.
This supports pensioners, sick members and children. The money
volved amounted to £39, and the committee decided to put the surplus
wards extra presents for children. There were complaints from some
members and we would like to know if our decision was legal.

A I must assume that your tote is run as a lottery under the Lotteries and
Amusements Act 1976, but you do not say whether it is a private scheme,
with sales of chances restricted to club members and other persons
attending the club, or whether non-members are allowed to participate, in which
case you would be required to register with the local authority under section 5 of
the Act.

If it was a private lottery, then the matter is dealt with in section 4 of the Act. If
a ticket is issued to participants, it must contain a statement that 'no prize won in
the lottery shall be paid or delivered by the promoters to any person other than the
person to whom the winning ticket was sold'. The club must abide by that
statement in its conduct of the lottery.

There is no corresponding restriction for societies' lotteries registered under
section 5, so that it would appear that no contravention of the lotteries laws would
occur if a prize was not distributed. The matter was raised by the Gaming Board
some time ago when they urged lottery promoters to make sure that they kept a
record of participants so that this situation could not occur.

Alternatively, the rules of your lottery should state that prizes must be claimed
within a certain time, otherwise they will be devoted to the purposes of the lottery,
i.e. the benevolent fund.

The subsequent action of your committee was, in the circumstances, perfectly
legal. It would have been more difficult to justify disposing of the money as
additional prizes to other winners, which I consider would contravene section 4
above. However, should a winner now come forward to claim a prize, you would be
put in a difficult position if the proceeds of the lottery have already been allocated.

QUESTIONS & ANSWERS ON CLUB LAW

13 Lottery accounts must be sent

Q I have recently taken over responsibility for our lottery competition and would like your advice on what procedures I have to adopt in dealing with the local authority and/or the Gaming Board in respect of this.

A It would appear that your lottery is a Society's Lottery run under section 5 of the Lotteries and Amusements Act 1976. It is a lottery promoted on behalf of a club or society which is established and conducted for the participation in or support of an athletic sport or game.

It is not a private club lottery, because tickets are on sale to members of the general public. Private lotteries among club members are covered by a different section and do not require registration with an outside body.

In your case, I assume that the club is registered with the local authority in respect of lotteries. The fee for registration is £35 and renewal on January 1 in each year costs a further £17.50.

Thereafter, if you run a lottery in which sales of tickets are made to the public, you must comply with certain conditions, including printing information about the promoter and the club on the ticket and making returns to the local authority in respect of any lottery which has been promoted.

It is a requirement of the Act that the promoter of the lottery should send a return within three months either to the local authority, in the case of a lottery where the total value of tickets is less than £20,000, or to the Gaming Board for Great Britain, where the ticket value is over that amount.

In fact, for larger lotteries the scheme under which the lottery is promoted must be registered with the Gaming Board before it starts, and the Board is authorised to require promoters to keep within specified limits with regard to expenses etc.

The charge for registering a scheme with the Board varies according to the size of lottery between £100 and £435. Registration of a society, however, currently costs £4600 with a renewal fee of £180.

The provisions of the Act allow you up to three months to submit returns to the local authority for lotteries of less than £20,000, but the Gaming Board expects accounts within six weeks of the lottery being held.

The Lotteries Regulations 1993 cover the sales of tickets and the composition of any scheme which has to be submitted to the Gaming Board. Tickets may not be sold in the street, or sold to persons under the age of 16.

14 Separate winning tickets

Q We have a thriving lottery with a number of agents/sellers in this area and we would like to ensure that the prizes are fairly distributed. But now our printers are refusing to let us have the winning tickets in a separate batch, so that we can make sure of this even distribution. Can we not insist on this?

A Although this may seem a fair system to you, it is open to abuse, as you must realise. Also, it is strictly against the law for you to make this request to your printer. Paragraph 11 of The Lotteries Regulations 1993 outlaws the practice of requiring winning tickets to be marked, identified or supplied separately.

It applies to 'scratch-off' and sealed lottery tickets, where the ticket itself would reveal whether it was a winner or not. Obviously, where you are using ordinary lottery tickets for which the prizes are drawn on a specified date, there is not the same problem, as the ticket cannot be identified as a 'winner' at the time of distribution or sale.

The printing industry has a code of practice to ensure security for lottery ticket printing, and if your supplier is a member of the group of printers covered by this, a code symbol appears on all tickets supplied to you. This indicates that the printer is following the approved code and will not supply or print tickets in contravention of the regulations.

Where winning tickets are supplied separately to the promoting organisation, any number of malpractices can result. For example, a dishonest helper can supply them to his friends, or they can be directed into one area, or even withdrawn from the distribution. This may not be happening at present in your case. but the regulations are designed to prevent the possibility. The regulations also cover overlapping lotteries, so that tickets in one lottery may not be sold more than three months before the date of a previous lottery, and include a rule banning multiple purchases in order to qualify for a prize.

15 Nil lottery return

Q We became registered with the local authority for a society's lottery under the Lotteries and Amusements Act 1976. We did not, however, get round to running any lotteries at all during the year. We have now received a very firm letter from the council, threatening legal action unless we make a return, and claiming that the Act requires us to do this. Can you advise?

A I can see no reason for a demand of this nature under the existing law. I can certainly not support the threats of further action which the council has made against the club.

Under paragraph 11 of Schedule 1 to the Lotteries and Amusements Act 1976, it is a requirement that the promoter of a lottery shall send a certified return not later than the end of the third month after the date of the lottery.

Any person who fails to send in such a return is, indeed, guilty of an offence. But it is clear that the intention of the Schedule is to allow for members of the public to study lottery returns, so that they can see where the money went, and that the proceeds were properly divided.

The local authority is obliged to keep returns for a period of at least 18 months, during which time they are open to inspection free of charge during office hours.

The requirement to send a return only applies to clubs which are registered with the local authority under Schedule 1 to the Act. Clubs which only run private lotteries among members, where tickets are not sold to the public, require no registration and do not need to give details of their own lotteries.

My advice is to send a brief letter to the council official concerned stating that you have held no lotteries, and end the matter there.

16 First was last

Q I was at another club function recently where my lottery ticket was first 'out of the hat.' I expected the main prize, a colour TV, only to be told on reaching the platform that the prizes were drawn in reverse order and I had won a plastic shopping bag. There was no indication that this would happen. How do I stand?

A Not very well! I should be most upset in your situation, and there must be a big legal question mark over this method of making the draw where it is not contained in the rules or in any announcement.

Your first recourse is to ask the promoter, whose name appears on the ticket, for a copy of the rules under which the lottery is run. You should also ask to see any announcement or other regulation which states that tickets are drawn in reverse order for prizes.

In a lottery, each ticket must have an equal chance of winning, and in one sense your 'winning' ticket has been disqualified from the chance of a major prize, unless it is returned to the draw after the distribution of the prize.

However, if the rules of the lottery cover this practice, your purchase of the ticket signifies your acceptance of those rules, and it would be difficult to gain any real recompense for what has happened.

My own view is that as this method has an element of unfairness in it, clubs should continue with the normal practice of drawing first for the major prize, or using a 'list' scheme, whereby tickets are matched against numbers and the relevant prize number is read out.

17 Card games

Q Our committee is in some doubt over the question of allowing dominoes, cribbage and brag to be played for money. Can such gaming be allowed? We are a registered club.

A Card games and other games played for money are not illegal in a members' club. I think your committee may be confusing the law on public houses with that applicable to clubs.

In pubs, only dominoes and cribbage are allowed for small stakes. A limited selection of other games may be permitted, at the discretion of the licensing justices.

In members' clubs, no such restrictions apply. There is no obligation to apply to the magistrates unless certain types of bankers' games such as pontoon or chemin de fer are contemplated. Equal chance gaming is allowed under Part I of the Gaming Act and as a club is a private place it is not affected by section 5 (which prohibits gaming in public places) or section 6 (which applies to licensed premises).

The club must make no levy on stakes or winnings, but it may charge a nominal 60p for participation in the gaming, if it is felt necessary.

The version of brag which may be allowed is the one where there is no bank and the players bet against each other. Bankers' games are specifically prohibited unless permitted under Part II of the Act.

Club committees should exercise extreme care that gaming is strictly controlled and does not get out of hand among the members.

18 Casino evenings as entertainment

Q We have been approached by a company offering to provide casino games equipment as part of a fixed-price package deal. They have literature which claims that this is within the law. Can you give us your opinion on this type of gaming?

A I have seen the literature from firms specialising in this form of entertainment. My own view is that as long as these evenings are properly run, they are legal under the present law.

The key to this lies in section 15 of the Lotteries and Amusements Act 1976. Although principally concerned with the conduct of lotteries, it does cover other types of gaming, including what is known as 'amusements with prizes at exempt entertainments'.

Where an entertainment such as a dinner, dance, bazaar, fete, sporting or athletic event is taking place, then gaming may be provided as an incidental part of the entertainment. This gaming may take the form of a lottery, or casino gaming, for prizes or money. The proceeds of the gaming, along with the proceeds of the whole entertainment, must not be devoted to purposes of private gain, but must go to charity or to club funds.

One other important point to bear in mind: the gaming must not be the only, or the only substantial, inducement to persons to attend the entertainment.

It is correct that this gaming equipment is offered to you on a fixed price basis. It is totally illegal to accept a deal involving a share of the profits from the entertainment or the gaming. The gaming must be conducted by or on behalf of the club, and the club must bear the loss or take the proceeds into funds.

This type of gaming may not be presented as a regular part of the club entertainment, nor should it be advertised as the main event or the principal attraction. That contravenes the section. It must be presented and treated as incidental to other activities.

It must be stressed that no members' club of your type can be turned into a casino under this section of the law. Games such as roulette are not, however, prohibited under this section, as long as the conditions outlined above are complied with.

19 Betting illegal

Q We recently ran a race night in the club which was highly successful. Now, one of our members has started running a similar scheme off his own bat with live televised racing during the afternoons. He acts as bookmaker for these occasions, saying that because it is a members' club it is a private bet and therefore not illegal. What is your view?

A My view is that this person is holding himself out as a bookmaker and the practice could land both him and the club in trouble if it is discovered.

The first thing to note is that race nights of the type you described are run on strictly controlled lines as a gaming amusement under the terms of the Lotteries and Amusements Act 1976. But placing bets with a member who is acting as bookmaker is not such an amusement, and contravenes the provisions of the Betting, Gaming and Lotteries Act 1963.

The fact that the club is a private place does not alter the illegality of the betting. It is illegal to use, cause or knowingly permit to be used any place which is not authorised for the placing of bets, or to pay out winnings or engage in any other 'betting transaction'.

The member does not appear to be operating on behalf of the club, but in his own right. He is not running a private lottery, as allowed by lotteries law, and he is not organising a form of gaming permitted by the Gaming Act. He is not licensed as a bookmaker, and even if he were, to conduct his business on the club premises would in itself be illegal.

I suggest that you put a stop to this practice at once, before the police discover what is happening and apply to the magistrates for a warrant to enter the club premises.

20 Winner must be present

Q One of our members has challenged the rule for our Sunday lunchtime draw that you must be in the club to receive a prize, or else the prize is drawn again. She says that it is illegal to cancel a winning ticket. This is just a small, cloakroom ticket type lottery and its intention is to get more members in at weekends. Is she right?

A As long as the condition is clearly explained in the rules, by announcement and on the ticket if possible, then it is perfectly lawful to stipulate that the winner must be present.

Lotteries and prize draws take many forms, some of which include special rules on qualification and attendance, or even more complicated conditions. As long as one set of participants is not prejudiced or has less of a chance of winning, then the draw 'with strings' is perfectly legal.

Members buy their tickets on the clear understanding that they or a representative must be present to claim a prize if it is drawn. The caller must give a reasonable time for the winning member to respond, after which he or she can re-draw the prize. The disappointed members can have no claim against the club if they fail to meet the conditions of the draw.

21 Wagers on pool

Q Can you settle an argument for us? I maintain that it is illegal for members to bet with one another on the outcome of games of pool played in the club. These members say that it is perfectly all right to have a private bet with one another. Who is right? The club is located on company property.

A I don't think that the location of the club makes any difference to the main issue, unless the company has a special rule forbidding betting, gaming and similar activities in social areas, which I doubt.

The simple fact is that a wager between two participants on the outcome of a sport or pastime is not illegal. It is not gaming and is not covered by betting, gaming or lotteries legislation.

Under the terms of the Gaming Act 1968, 'gaming' means the playing of a game of chance for winnings in money or money's worth, even if the person who is participating is not risking any money to take part.

The essential aspect of this is the definition of a 'game of chance'. The same Act states clearly that it 'does not include any athletic game or sport', but includes a game of chance and skill combined.

While it is accepted that in many sports there are chance events, especially in table games such as pool or snooker, the main principle on which the game is decided is the skill of the competitors. It follows therefore that the game is not a game of chance as defined in the Act and that wagering among participants on the outcome is not gaming.

Betting on the outcome by non-participants is, however, quite another matter. They are not taking part in an athletic game or sport, but are wagering on the outcome of an event over which they have no control. If such wagering is organised in any way, e.g. by having a stockholder or bookkeeper, or laying odds, then technically this could infringe the Betting, Gaming and Lotteries Act.

22 No need to register

Q We have started to run a special numbers game for members recently, where they participate on a weekly basis. I enclose details of the scheme and would ask you two questions. Do we need to notify the local authority of this under our registration for the Betting, Gaming and Lotteries Act, and are the takings in this game subject to VAT?

A The scheme which you describe to me seems certainly to be a private lottery, run under the terms of section 4 of the Lotteries and Amusements Act 1976. This allows for draws or sweepstakes to be held exclusively among members of a club, and guests or members of the public are specifically excluded.

You have sent me details of your previous registration with the local authority. This appears to relate to fund-raising lotteries which you have run where tickets or chances were sold by members to their families and the public.

It is true that in such circumstances returns do have to be made within a specified time, giving details of the amount collected as stakes and returned as prizes, together with the date or dates of the lottery. But this scheme for members is not a 'society's lottery' within the meaning of the Lotteries and Amusements Act 1976, which is the current law on the subject. No returns need to be made to the local authority in respect of this lottery.

As for your second question, VAT is not chargeable on the operation of any lottery, and from the description you have given to me, it would appear that this is a form of lottery and as such is exempt from VAT, as with other forms of raffle within the club.

Chapter 15
Gaming machines

1 Different certificates

Q I am still confused about the business of club registration, particularly for fruit machines. Does the registration from the magistrates (which we have until 2004) cover us for machines as well, or does the annual licence from Customs and Excise do that?

A I am not surprised that some club officials are confused by the amount of licences and certificates which they seem to need. For this reason, this book contains a checklist at Appendix A, to which you should refer.

First, I must make it clear that drink and gaming machines are two different matters — and they both need a certificate from the magistrates.

Forget about the annual licence duty for a moment. As well as paying a hefty fee for the privilege of having your jackpot machines, you must have a certificate of registration in respect of gaming on your premises.

The form which you should hold will be headed 'Certificate of Registration under Part III (or Part II) of the Gaming Act 1968'.

A certificate under Part III is for machines only. Most members' clubs of your type are only registered under Part III, because they want jackpot machines and their other gaming is confined to bingo sessions and occasional lotteries among members, for which the additional registration under Part II is not required (*see previous chapter for details*).

The registration which currently covers you until 2004 is for the supply of liquor. You have been granted a ten-year certificate from June 1994 under the terms of the Licensing Act 1964. This is the authority for the club bar. It has nothing to do with gaming machines and certainly does not operate to allow their use on the club premises.

Registration under Part III of the Gaming Act 1968 lasts for **five** years from the date of registration. Renewal of this certificate will probably be at a different date from renewal of your registration for the supply of liquor. You should keep a note of both dates in a prominent place.

In addition, you have to pay an annual licence duty per machine. For this, you will receive a form of licence from Customs and Excise, stating that you have paid the required duty. The licence itself does not authorise the premises to be used — it merely authorises the machines.

2 Responsibility for renewal

Q We are a registered club with two jackpot machines. Recently our supplier asked us about our registration renewal, which we replied was his responsibility. It has since been discovered that our certificate has expired. Could you explain what our responsibilities are in this, as we have had a change of committee in the past year?

A Club officials must realise that, in general, they are responsible for ensuring that all documents, licences, certificates and other authorisations are in order.

The reason that your supplier expressed an interest in your certificate of registration was that he is under an obligation *not* to supply you with jackpot machines unless you hold the necessary authorisation. It is his business to ensure that he complies with the Gaming Act, and the Gaming Board would take a dim view if he continued to supply you without checking your certificate.

But it is the club and *not* the supplier which makes the application to the local licensing authority, which is a committee of the licensing justices for your area. Details of the methods of application for renewal are laid out in Schedule 7 to the Gaming Act 1968.

In your case, the certificate has expired, so you cannot make application within the specified period, which is not earlier than three months and not later than *six weeks* before it is due to expire.

However, the court can entertain a late application if your failure was due to inadvertence and you make the application within an extended period which they may allow. The application must be signed by the chairman or secretary of the club — the supplier has nothing to do with it.

Remember that registration for gaming machines lasts for **five years only**. Registration for liquor (or for gaming under Part II) may last for a period of up to **ten years**. Do not confuse the two.

3 How many machines?

Q Can you tell me how many jackpot machines we are allowed to have in this club? We currently have two but someone has told me that the limit has been increased. We have a registration under Part III of the Gaming Act.

A The limit on machine numbers was indeed increased in 1996 for all types of clubs and casinos. In place of the fixed number of two machines for all establishments, there are now different limits, depending on the type of operation.

As the law now stands, registered clubs and miners' welfare institutes are allowed a maximum of three jackpot machines; commercial bingo clubs are allowed four such machines; and casinos may have up to ten. Bingo clubs may in future be allowed to mix jackpot and AWP machines, which has previously been prohibited.

Many clubs find that two machines is sufficient, particularly with the high level of duty. But an extra one would be allowed.

4 Failure to pay out

Q Can you give us a ruling on the question of a gaming machine failing to pay out? Is the steward obliged to pay the person from the bar till, or can we insist on a committee member verifying the amount and paying it later if necessary?

A Under the terms of the Gaming Act 1968, the only benefit or advantage which the player of a gaming machine is entitled to receive is a 'a coin or coins delivered by the machine'.

In their report for 1974, the Gaming Board recognised the problem of machines which failed to pay out, but they re-stated the law that as the Gaming Act was specific on this point, if the machine failed to pay out, the prize was lost and the player was not legally entitled to be reimbursed from any other source.

However, the Board also tacitly acknowledged the difficulty of enforcing this strictly by saying that they would not expect their inspectors to initiate a prosecution against clubs which contravened this strict rule by making a payment over the bar or from other club funds, as long as the machine was immediately taken out of service until the fault was rectified.

The Board has also commented critically on machine operators who deliberately keep the payout chutes under-filled so that the likelihood of a full jackpot or prize payout is restricted. Clubs should ensure that their machines do not fall into this category.

In the circumstances you describe, therefore, you should point out the legal position to members and attempt to draw up clear instructions in the event of this happening. It would certainly be acceptable to have the claim verified, as casual payouts from the bar till could cause stock check problems and should be avoided wherever possible.

5 Machines in new clubroom

Q This club holds a registration certificate in respect of a clubhouse in the main offices and the sportsground, which is several miles away. There are two jackpot gaming machines at the sportsground, and it has now been proposed that a further one be installed at the clubhouse. What is the legal position?

A There appears to be nothing in the gaming laws to prevent a club which has two entirely separate premises from exceeding the normal limit of three machines allowed under the Gaming Act 1968.

In order to operate jackpot machines, a club must be registered under this Act. Application for machine registration is made to the licensing justices responsible for betting and gaming for the petty sessions area in which the premises where the machines are installed are situated.

There is no provision in the Gaming Act comparable to that in the Licensing Act which allows a club to be registered in respect of two entirely different premises, as indeed your club is for the supply of liquor. The procedure therefore seems to be for you to apply for a **second** registration for gaming machines under Part III of the Gaming Act to the justices who cover your head office location.

This would mean that you held two registrations for machines. But they would be for different premises in different licensing areas. That is perfectly in order. It would, in effect, mean that you could have up to three machines in each location.

6 Not members of the public

Q It has been maintained by one of our committee members that as guests are technically members of the public they are not permitted to play the gaming machines. Our rules do not cover this point, but we have two jackpot machines and have been told that the public must not play them. What is the position of guests?

A The law does not, in fact, state that jackpot machines may only be played by members of the club which is registered for their use. The relevant section of the Gaming Act 1968 contains the condition that such machines may not be used on premises 'at any time when the public have access, whether on payment or otherwise'.

If it were true that guests are to be considered members of the public, then any club which permitted guests at all would *never* be allowed to have jackpot machines in operation, by virtue of this quotation from the Gaming Act.

On the contrary, it has for a long time been held that *genuine* guests of individual members are not members of the public for the purposes of the law. The club continues to remain a private place, even though these non-members are allowed access to the premises.

So the question of whether they are permitted to play the machines is purely one for internal club administration. The committee could decide that the machines should be for the use of members only, and may place a notice to that effect, if it reflects the wishes of the members.

Any guests would have to abide by that ruling while on the premises and may be asked to leave if they break it.

7 Separate machine account

Q This is a members' club with Part III registration under the Gaming Act for machines only. We do not have other types of gaming. The police are saying that it is the justices' policy to insist on a separate bank account for machine takings which is open to inspection. Is this a legal requirement?

A This is a matter which has come up on several occasions in the past, but clearly still surfaces from time to time. I consider it inappropriate to make such a demand from a genuine members' club such as yours.

The reason for the stipulation is presumably for the magistrates to ensure that the proceeds from gaming machines can be scrutinized to ensure that they go to the members and not to other purposes of private gain. This is only appropriate in the case of proprietary or semi-proprietary clubs where there could be some commercial profit being made.

The problem lies in the wider interpretation of Part III of the Gaming Act, which affords a route for certain proprietary clubs to have machines by means of registration. Although intended for genuine members' clubs only, a court ruling allowed certain profit-making clubs to apply as long as the proceeds of the machines were devoted 'to purposes other than private gain'.

If the money was put into the general account of the club, it was thought that it could not be checked to see if the members benefited. So certain magistrates' courts devised the ideas of imposing a condition that there should be a separate bank account.

But all the money which goes into the account of a genuine members' club is used for the benefit of the members as a whole. There is not private gain in a club such as yours, and cannot be under the rules which you have enclosed. It is therefore wholly unreasonable to insist on the setting up of a separate account, when the machine proceeds are clearly shown on your balance sheet and the surplus goes into the general funds of the club.

There is no legal authority for the making of this demand, certainly not on renewal of registration. You should oppose this request, for the reasons given above.

8 Machines off?

Q This club has two gaming machines. One of our committee has suggested that the machines should be switched off by a master switch operated from the bar at 11 p.m., the time when the bar closes and no more drinks are served. Others want the machines on as long as the club is open. Can you tell us whether there is any law on this?

A There is no requirement that gaming machines operated on premises in respect of which a club is registered should be only made available for play during the permitted hours for the supply of drink.

Those permitted hours apply only to the supply and consumption of intoxicating liquor, for which your club appears to be registered. The club is undoubtedly also registered for gaming machines under Part III of the Gaming Act 1968. This is a different registration and you hold a different certificate in respect of it.

Nothing on that certificate or in the Gaming Act itself, suggests that machines have to be switched off. The only time restriction on gaming is for casino gaming clubs which are not allowed to open at certain times on Sundays.

This being said, it is a sensible idea to have some form of byelaw or committee policy on the use of machines, especially if the responsibility is to be given to the steward or some other club servant. If a policy is reached, it should be made clear to members, so that they know the machines will not be available at certain times.

9 Proprietary machines

Q I have read with interest that a proprietary club owner has been registered under Part III of the Gaming Act. We would like to have machines here, and have a number of club conditions attached to our licence. What do we have to do to get jackpot machines?

A The Act gives a more or less absolute discretion to the magistrates to register or not to register clubs which are not bona fide members' clubs. By their nature, proprietary clubs are not such clubs. They are owned and managed, for the most part, by a proprietor. Such control as he gives to the members is his own affair. He can withdraw it again, if he so desires. The members have no real rights or interest in the club or its financial affairs.

Perhaps it would best be illustrated by imagining one of your members walking into your office and asking to see your books. In certain genuine members' clubs, this is a right. Of course, in your own case, you run a commercial enterprise and would refuse such a request.

Registration has been refused to many clubs which are proprietary in nature. However, courts have entertained applications from proprietors when they have been able to show that the direction of the revenue from gaming machines is under the control of a members' committee and that the profits are devoted to enhancing or improving the club and its facilities, for the overall benefit of the members.

This means, in effect, keeping separate accounts, using the money for improvements, asking members for their views, and in some cases having an appointed official to open the machine and remove the takings. Certain courts have made it possible for proprietary clubs to have machines of this type by laying down guidelines on the method of accounting for, and disposing of, the profits in this way.

My view is that the presentation of an application for registration in these circumstances is best done by a specialist solicitor who understands what the magistrates are seeking.

10 Collecting machine cash

Q Can you tell us who should legally be allowed to open the gaming machines and take the money out of them in a members' club? How should this be organised?

A This question is important from an administrative point of view, as well as from a legal one. In fact, the Gaming Act has a separate section devoted to this very subject. It applies to any machine under Part III of the Act which is installed on premises which are licensed under the Gaming Act, or in a club or miners' welfare institute which is registered under the Act.

In the case of registered clubs, the persons authorised are:

'...any officer or member of the club and any person employed by or on behalf of the members of the club in connection with the premises'.

This does *not* include the machine supplier or his agent, the repair man or other outside individual. But it would, of course, include the club steward and any other committee member duly authorised by the committee to remove money from the machines.

It seems to me imperative that all clubs have a clear system for the taking and banking of machine cash. It should never be left to an individual and is much better done by an official and one other member of the committee, or an independent club member to ensure that the money goes in the right direction.

Where ready cash of this nature is concerned, it forms such a temptation that each 'opening' should be carried out, if possible, in a formal manner. Jackpot machines now have meters for checking purposes, so that any major shortfall should become immediately apparent.

It is also foolish to allow too many key-holders, for whatever reason. If the steward holds one, he should be issued with clear instructions as to how and when he may use it, and for what purpose. All machine openings should be logged in some way, and at least two responsible persons should be present.

It is best if all cash from machines is banked, rather than used for other purposes, except perhaps as immediate change, for which notes or cheques are substituted at the time. The amount should be checked and agreed by all those who are present and responsible to the club for this activity.

11 Machine choice

Q I have recently taken over a club in this town and would like to know whether I can have both jackpot machines and the pub-style machines, as long as I only have two of the first kind. I could put them in different parts of the club, if this is necessary. Would I need two licences?

A I am sorry to disappoint you, but you must make a choice. It is either up to three of the jackpot type club machines, or a permitted number of the other type of machines.

It will depend on whether you have taken over a club with existing gaming facilities, or are starting from scratch. This will affect the type of authority you require and the type of machine made available.

At present, I assume that you hold a club liquor licence in your own name, or that of a nominee. You have the choice, therefore, of registration under Part III of the Gaming Act, or application for a permit under section 34 of the Act.

In the first instance, you would be allowed a maximum of three jackpot machines. The court has a discretionary power to grant or refuse application by proprietary clubs for registration under this Part of the Act, and it may be that they impose certain conditions or ask for certain information about what is to be done with the revenue from the machines.

As far as permits for amusement with prizes machines are concerned, these are granted by the local licensing justices, who renew your liquor licence each year. This type of machine is strictly limited as to the type and amount of awards or prizes it may pay out; currently the cash limit is £25.

Clubs which are licensed under Part II of the Gaming Act are entitled to make a choice between jackpot machines or amusement-type machines, by virtue of section 32 of the Act. Licensed bingo clubs, however, are to be allowed a mixture of machine types.

12 Drayman's luck

Q The other day, during the morning session, one of the draymen played the gaming machine while I was checking stock. He won a minor jackpot, but I pointed out that the machine was for members. He insisted on keeping the money at first, but then handed most of it back, under pressure. Was I right?

A One has to ask what a drayman was doing in the club bar at that time of the day anyway, but let that pass. The legal position is that the machine and its contents belong to the members of the club collectively. It is illegal to have a jackpot machine available for play at any time when members of the public have access to the premises.

The drayman was not entitled to play your machine (unless he was a club member, which appears not to be the case); he was therefore not entitled to walk off with his 'winnings'.

You do not enclose your rules, and it may be that they fail to specify who may play the machines. If so, then both members and guests may play, and guests may take the jackpot if they win it. It would be illegal to allow guests to play the machine, but forbid them from taking the jackpot.

Taking of any money from the club by this drayman was therefore technically theft—as much as if he had opened the back of the machine and removed money from it that way.

I recommend that you place a large notice by the machine stating 'members and guests only'. That way, any other person playing the machine will be aware that he does so illegally, and therefore has no rights over any money which accrues to him.

13 Doubtful supplier

Q We have recently held discussions with a local businessman who deals with amusement machines, among other things. He has said that we can have one of the brand new £250 machines in the club on a strict 50/50 basis, with him supplying the machine and splitting the proceeds straight down the middle. He says the machine will only be opened with the secretary or treasurer present. Should we go ahead on this basis? There is nothing in writing.

A It sounds from your letter as if this man dabbles in a number of things and is not directly a certificated supplier of gaming machines. Certainly, what he proposes is strictly illegal.

Under the terms of the Gaming Act 1968, the supply of gaming machines to a club which is registered under Part II or Part III of that Act must be made either by a certificated supplier or the representative or agent of such a supplier. Persons who do not hold a Gaming Board certificate are therefore not allowed to make deals on machines with clubs.

The second point is that profit-sharing is illegal. There must be a fixed rental or hire-purchase agreement for such machines. The supplier is not authorised to open the cash box — only a duly-authorised official of the club is allowed to do this.

In spite of regular warnings by the Gaming Board, there are still people who deal illegally in gaming machines, or who seek to make arrangements with clubs which are specifically outlawed by the Gaming Act. New machines of this type are available from regular, reliable sources at terms which are far more favourable to the club and you would be well advised to contact one of the reputable suppliers to find out the level of rental which you would expect to pay for such a machine.

Chapter 16
Entertainment and copyright

1 Refund for cancelled artistes

Q Last month we held a dance at our clubhouse, which was only advertised within the company. Members and guests were admitted on payment of a £2 entrance fee. The advertised band failed to turn up, but we managed to obtain a substitute entertainer. Now, one of the committee says that his guests want their money back. We have offered £2 off any future function. Are we in the right?

A Although this is a situation which occurs rather too often in clubs, with artistes failing to turn up, the question of refunds is more difficult to determine. A great deal depends on the type of contract made with the member or with the guest, and the nature of the entertainment.

In your case, I consider that a full refund is not required. The member and his guests may have been disappointed at the non-appearance of the band, but they remained for the entertainment and it is clear that the presence of the band was not their *sole* reason for attending.

Where a star act is billed and the price of admission is geared to that performer, it could well be argued that the club is bound to make a full refund or offer entrance at a reduced price, because the contract was made for that performer.

But where a more general entertainment is advertised, such as a dance, it would be more difficult for the guests to claim that the whole contract had been frustrated. This is especially true as they 'consented' to a variation of the contract by remaining for the alternative entertainment.

The situation in your own case is also complicated by the very nature of the contract — and it is something which all members' clubs should bear in mind.

The committee of the club is acting on behalf of the membership as a whole, and in certain senses the only contractual liability it incurs the same as all other members. Strictly speaking, the disappointed guests may only have recourse to the member who introduced them, as they should not have any contractual relationship with the club.

According to your rules, 'every visitor shall be considered the guest of ... the member introducing him or her...' which means that there is no direct contract and their entrance fee should have been paid by the member himself. He is subject to the rules of the club and the decision of the committee. You are therefore perfectly entitled to make this goodwill offer in the circumstances.

2 Club music is public

Q We do not not have any juke box or background music in our club, but we do have a television set in the bar and a radio for the steward. I have been told that we need a licence from the Performing Right Society, but have not seen one of these. We have a TV licence already. Is this enough?

A The playing of any kind of music by radio or television constitutes a 'public' performance under the Copyright Design and Patents Act. It has been held that although the club premises are not public in the accepted sense, the listeners are public in terms of the performance. This fine legal point has assisted the Performing Right Society to continue demanding annual licence fees from non-profit making members' clubs.

I am afraid it makes no difference if you do not have any live music, or juke box on the premises. It will also do no good to maintain that the members only watch sports programmes. Even the signature tunes and jingles used on television may be subject to copyright, and you will have to pay.

The PRS rates are based on agreed fees for many types of premises. Sometimes the level of these fees has been subject to legal challenge — successfully in 1991 when it was held that an increased tariff rate was not justified. But in certain cases where clubs provide live entertainment or a great deal of music, such as in discotheques, the situation becomes more complicated and a higher fee may be demanded.

Usually, the club will be approached direct by the PRS. Failure to take out a licence will eventually result in legal action by the Society and an injunction to prevent infringement of copyright until a licence is acquired.

3 Forms to fill

Q We have been contacted on several occasions by the Performing Right Society concerning the completion of programme forms for our club. They appear to want us to write down the titles, arrangers, times performed and the date of each performance of *all* tunes performed on our premises. We do not engage musicians directly; they are hired through an entertainment agency. What is the legal position?

A The Performing Right Society exists to collect royalties for the public performance of musical works. Their policy is to distribute the money they collect (after deducting the costs of administering the scheme, which are considerable) to the individual members of the society whose works are performed.

They produce a licence which is, in fact, a form of contract and is not like a television or driving licence. Among the conditions of this contract is one that the club undertakes to supply the information you have mentioned in the form of returns, which must be posted back to them.

Obviously, the club secretary or entertainments manager cannot possibly know this information personally. It has therefore become accepted practice to hand the forms over to the performers for completion. But the performers are not obliged to complete them and the time-consuming chore is often a matter of disagreement within the club itself.

The legal, as opposed to the practical, position is that the making of returns does constitute a condition of the licence and that your predecessor as secretary signed this licence, thereby completing a contract with the PRS. At first, they did not enforce the condition, but now they are seeking to do so. The licence gives them the right to cancel it if the conditions are not fulfilled, and presumably they would then sue the club if it continued to provide musical entertainment.

In view of the thousands of musical performances given annually in clubs, it may seem amazing that every single tune should have to be noted down; but that appears to be the Society's policy and you may find yourselves compelled to comply eventually.

4 Reassessment demand

Q We have recently received from the Performing Right Society a form entitled 'Reassessment Form J'. Can you tell us whether we are obliged to supply all this detailed information and under what statute these people are authorised to make this demand?

A The authority for making this demand from clubs is contained in the contract which exists between the club and the Society. In the contract, which is the licence authorising the club to play copyright music 'in public', the PRS reserves the right to request certain returns to be made to them, so that they can ascertain what music is being played, by what means and at what functions.

I assume that all this new information on such items as video projectors and video jukeboxes will enable them to charge a higher licence fee to clubs. I note also that the form asks for full details of 'events open to the general public', which is a highly dubious entry for registered members' clubs to complete, as it is clearly established that members of the public are not allowed to use private club facilities.

If you are dissatisfied with the assessment of your fee by the PRS, there is an appeals procedure to a special tribunal.

5 Licence for recordings

Q I have recently been approached by an organisation calling itself Phonographic Performance. They have threatened to take me to court unless I pay them an annual licence fee for the records and tapes I use. Can they do this? I already pay a large fee to the PRS for music.

A I am afraid that you will have to pay this licence fee if you wish to continue playing records and tapes in your club. The company concerned, Phonographic Performance Limited, has a right under the Copyright, Designs and Patents Act 1988 to authorise clubs and other places to give public performances of recorded music only on payment of a licence fee.

A public performance has the same meaning as for the Performing Right Society. Even though a club is a private place, the members are considered to be 'a public' for the purposes of this Act.

There is no doubt that PPL will have recourse to the courts in much the same way that the PRS has done over the years to protect their interests. They are in fact becoming more active in asserting their legal rights.

If you look carefully on the CD, record label or cassette sleeve you will see small print stating that public performance of the material without authority is prohibited. PPL exists to safeguard the rights of the copyright holders in the recording, apart from the rights of the composers and arrangers, which are covered by the PRS fee you already pay.

As with PRS, charges are based on a tariff which takes into account the amount of recorded music used in the club. Recorded music received as part of a broadcast is not directly included.

6 Video film shows

Q What is our position if we show video films with a 50p charge to members and bona fide guests? We do not advertise outside the club premises, but certain members of the committee have queried the charge.

A First of all a club is quite at liberty to make a charge to members for special facilities, such as film shows. The club is also entitled to charge for the guest, but strictly speaking this should be paid by the introducing member. Additional charges are quite lawful in members' clubs if members wish to make use of particular items or attend particular functions. Free access at all times is not a legal requirement.

The big question mark is over the showing of the films themselves. You do not give me details of the source of your films, but you should be aware of the increasing interest in the matter of non-copyright and 'pirate' video tapes which are now being distributed.

A club is not in any special position with regard to the copyright in these films. Cassettes for home use, for example, although sold or rented in large numbers from high street shops, are not licensed for club showing. According to the terms of rental, found printed on the covers, the films are hired for home use only and should not be shown in clubs or to a paying audience.

The fact that a members' club is a private place does not exclude it from the Copyright, Design and Patents Act. In this respect, a club is in the same position as a public house, hotel or other establishment where people gather.

The important thing is to check that the films which you show are copyright-free. If you have a special supplier, ask him. If you are renting these cassettes from a local source, check that you are not inadvertently infringing copyright. Read the small print on the rental agreement or cassette case. This may well show you where you are going wrong.

7 Licence for videograms

Q This club holds a cinema licence in respect of our disco screen. Now I have been approached by an organisation claiming that I need *another* licence from them in respect of showing pop cassettes, which they call 'videograms'. The material I get has been copyright cleared by the suppliers. What should be my response?

A It seems that the situation with regard to video is developing in the same dual-copyright way as for music (*see previous answers in this chapter*). Most club owners are now aware that one organisation operates on behalf of the copyright holders in the musical works, while another operates in respect of the copyright records or cassettes on which the music is played.

Until recently, video material such as feature films was jealously protected by the major film distributors, who would not grant any form of 'licence' for video showing of their major releases at all, and threatened to prosecute clubs who tried to show such films which they had hired from the local video shop.

But the increasing number of specially-recorded video cassettes and the growing market for the commercial use of video has clearly persuaded manufacturers that there is money to be made from royalty payments for the use of this material by way of a copyright 'licence'.

This is now administered by an organisation called Video Performance Limited, which operates from the same address and telephone number as Phonographic Performance in London. They will issue their own form of licence, authorising you to use video cassettes produced by their members, on payment of an annual licence fee.

As with the music copyright organisations, this is not an official government licence, but a contract, permitting you to use copyright material on payment. The relevant organisation fixes the contract terms and also fixes the level of licence fee.

There are some companies who advertise themselves as being able to provide programmes which are 'copyright free' or 'copyright cleared' direct to you. Such claims must be thoroughly examined. Video piracy still abounds, and it may be that the company with whom you are dealing has itself received copyright material from an unauthorised source. Your best recourse initially is to ask your supplier whether the cassettes or DVDs which you received are authorised for group showing and whether any copyright fee is included in the price which you pay.

8 Cinema licence needed?

Q Is a cinema licence needed for our club? We are a registered members' club, but we do have a video on which we show films from time to time, but mainly use it for live sporting events and football etc.

A A cinema licence under the Cinemas Act 1985 is required for any film exhibition, which is defined as 'any exhibition of moving pictures' except live or cable television. However, the licence is only required where there is an element of private gain involved in the showing. Clubs and societies are specifically exempt under the Act and therefore there is no need for you to obtain such a licence.

Proprietary clubs on the other hand, unless they can prove that they are providing an 'exempt exhibition' to which members of the public are not admitted, would probably require such a licence from the local authority.

9 Late cabaret

Q Can you tell me whether it is against the terms of our club registration to allow entertainment to continue after the end of permitted hours, whether we have an extension or not?

A What normally happens is that the entertainment ends when the bar closes, but this need not be the case. If the club permits the entertainment to continue, then as long as the permitted hours are complied with, the show can go on.

The only problem that I can see is the possibility of attracting attention late at night when it is known that your bar should be closed. The police might feel suspicious if sounds of entertainment were continuing well past the terminal hour, and this could lead to a police raid on the premises, or at least an exploratory visit. They might then not be satisfied with your explanation that the bar is already closed. But if it is, and no illegal consumption is taking place, then the police have no case against you.

The only other problem could be nuisance and disturbance to neighbours, which is a matter either for the police or the local authority inspectors, if a complaint is made.

Clubs should recognise that it is not a legal requirement that the premises should be closed outside permitted hours. Clubs can open 24 hours a day, if necessary. It is only the bar which must be closed at specific times.

10 Annoying the neighbours

Q This club has been operating on its present site for more than 30 years. We have disco-style entertainment two nights a week for the younger members, by popular demand. Recently, a couple moved into a house close to the club. The previous occupier never complained, but they have reported us to the local council, saying the music is too loud. The houses were built well after the club was opened. Have they the right to stop our music?

A The fact that the club has been on the same site for a length of time will not affect its obligations under the legislation which covers disturbance of this kind.

The Environmental Protection Act 1990 does allow the local authority to take action against individuals or companies which create a nuisance through pollution of some kind. Noise is one aspect of this type of pollution, which may disturb local residents.

In the vast majority of cases, there is no need for prosecution, because the environmental health officers seek to work out some form of compromise in the dispute. This is what has started in your case.

Once a complaint has been made, the officers are bound to make enquiries.

They may not at first stop the music, but seek to limit it in some way, often by asking the club to fit a limiting device on the sound output. There is no statutory decibel level above which an offence is committed, although local authorities do have guidelines. There can be no hard and fast rule on this, as so many factors are involved.

The noise is the club's responsibility and not that of the group. As you are well aware, most pop groups like to play at a sound level above that which is reasonably required for audibility. But it is also true that a limiter can be a great annoyance when it cuts out on 'peaks'.

A local council officer has no statutory right to set a noise limiter in your club. If you do obtain one, the equipment is your property and has been acquired presumably so that you can avoid the risk of prosecution.

It would seem that the local authority has not yet issued a formal notice to the club requiring it to abate the nuisance. This is usually the first step if a compromise cannot be reached by negotiation or discussion. It may be that the EHO does not think the noise is excessive. If he does, then you ought to take some steps to limit it.

The club is permitted to appeal against any abatement notice to a magistrates' court within 21 days of receiving it.

11 Is an entertainments licence needed?

Q We are a members' club and I enclose for your information a copy of a letter received recently demanding a fee for an entertainments licence from the local authority. As far as I am aware we have never had one before. Is this a new law, and how does it affect our Saturday night dances/discos etc.?

A In general, clubs such as yours are not open to the public, and legislation affecting 'public' access will not apply to you. This entertainment licence is the responsibility of district councils under the Local Government (Miscellaneous Provisions) Act 1982, and in your case the London borough council, which operates under a separate Act.

It may be that the council has noticed that you promote dances and has assumed that these will require a licence. But of course, if they are simply club activities, open only to members and bona fide guests, as they should be, then members of the public are not admitted and the entertainment will not be considered 'public' under the Act.

In a case decided under the previous legislation in 1968 it was held that guests of members of a bona fide club were not members of the public and that a licence of this type was not required for their entertainment.

The fact that you advertise the dances locally in the paper would only be material if the advertisements were directed at the public and not at your own membership who live locally. If, however, you admit persons on payment on the door, without any formality, then not only will you be in breach of the Act but you may fall foul of the licensing law as well.

I note that under your club rules there is no provision for the admission of persons other than members and their guests except as visitors in accordance with strict rules concerning sporting events. There is, therefore, no way in which members of the public may legally gain admission to dances, except as guests of members in the normal way, being signed in under your rules.

If you do make sales to non-members from the bar at these events, you risk the possibility of police action against you, or a complaint against the registration certificate.

You should respond to the claim for an entertainments licence fee by stating that you are a private members' club not open to the public and that accordingly a licence is not being applied for because it is not required.

12 Licence for dances?

Q We are a registered club and hire out our hall for local events such as weddings, anniversaries and birthdays etc. My question is: although the club does not normally need an entertainments licence would we need one for this type of event on our premises?

A From your rules, and from the nature of the events in question, it is clear that the persons attending the events for which you let your hall are not entitled to enter merely on payment of an entrance fee; they are guests attending an event restricted to persons invited by the organiser.

It is also clear that the club is not responsible for providing the entertainment.

That, too, is up to the organisers of the individual events. The functions therefore appear to me to be 'private', in the sense that they are not open to any member of the public who wishes to enter.

I would consider commercial letting in a quite different light. If the club hires out the hall for, say, a discotheque which is freely advertised in the locality and to which any local resident can come, then this would indeed be a public entertainment, and anyone who 'provided' the entertainment would need a licence for it. Also, an offence is committed not only by the person or persons organising the entertainment, but by anyone who 'lets the place or otherwise makes it available'. This would mean the club.

13 Sunday dancing

Q I am concerned that we may be at a disadvantage in this club. Our licence states that we may only have music on Sundays, but I have heard that the law has now been changed to allow both music and dancing. Is this true and can we change our licence?

A The restriction on Sunday activities comes from section 3 of the Sunday Entertainments Act 1932, which does state that the local licensing authority has the power to grant licences 'in respect only of musical entertainments on Sundays'.

However, the law has been changed to disapply the Sunday Observance Act to public dancing on Sundays, which has opened the way for clubs and other licensed premises to apply for a variation of the public entertainment licence (PEL) to allow dancing and so extend the operation of their special hours certificate.

While the 1932 Act still technically applies, most if not all local authorities are following the goverment's own lead and not prohibiting dancing on Sundays. But you must apply for a variation to have this 'music only' condition removed.

Incidentally, I notice that you are essentially a members' club, so I wonder why you need a **public** entertainment licence in the first place? This is normally only applicable to commercial licensed premises and not to members' clubs.

14 Charge for entry

Q We are a private works sports and social club with our own sports field, on which is situated a small clubhouse. We would like to put entertainment on, but are told we cannot charge admission as we only have the one bar. In November we had a bonfire and disco and made a charge at the gate. Is there any way we can make a charge for the clubhouse?

A You do not make it clear who 'told' you that it was not possible to make a charge on the door at the clubhouse. It would appear to me that nothing in your rules prevents this from being done.

There is no law which says that all the facilities offered by a club to its members must be free. Indeed, it is only by the mutual pooling of resources from members to the club that any social club exists at all.

The manner in which money is transferred from the individual members into club funds is something to be decided either by the membership in general meeting, or by the club committee, in the interests of the membership as a whole. If they decide that for certain facilities an entrance charge or participation fee will be required, then that is perfectly legal.

Obviously, if the ordinary member is being denied the facilities of the club in a material way, he has a right to complain. If, for example, you ran a disco every night of the week and forced every member to pay the entrance charge, this would undoubtedly lead to protests. It would not necessarily be in the best interests of the membership as a whole.

The fact that your facilities are limited, so that any special entertainment which you provide must of necessity occupy the only principal room of the club, creates difficulties. But it does not mean that charging for periodic entertainment is against the law.

If you are in any doubt, it would be best to raise the matter at the next annual general meeting, or at a special meeting called to discuss the issue. This will allow you to gain the general opinion of members. If the feeling is that entertainment should be provided, then you may make a charge as and when these events occur. It would be polite to give a warning to ordinary members that a door charge will be in operation that night.

15 Numbered tickets at the door

Q Is it a legal requirement that entry tickets to a nightclub have to be numbered? I have been told that I could be breaking the law if we just hand out plain printed cards that don't have a number on them.

A This is not so much a question of a legal requirement as much as the result of a condition imposed upon the entertainment licence by the local authority.

There is no legal provision which would require admission tickets to be issued at all, so there is little likelihood of numbering being compulsory.

If you operate as a club, then it may be that the liquor licence which covers the club stipulates that only members and their guests may be admitted, so that membership cards should be issued and be shown at the door. These may need to be numbered, in order to keep a check on membership.

However, clearly the issuing of a ticket is a useful device for keeping a check on the number of persons admitted to the premises on a particular evening. There has for many years been concern by public health and fire authorities on the matter of overcrowding, and in most cases the entertainment licence — and sometimes the registration certificate — stipulates the maximum number of persons allowed on the premises, or in specified parts of the premises, at any one time.

It might be that the numbering of tickets for admission gives an instant indication of the number of persons who might be on the premises. Both the police and public health officials would expect the proprietor or his representative to be able to produce an indication of how many people were in the building, to ensure that the limit imposed on the licence was not being exceeded.

16 Fire inspection

Q We have recently been told that we may be liable to a fire inspection by the local fire authority, because we show children's films once a month. We make no money out of this: it's just a service to the local kids. Is this right?

A I note from your rules that you operate as a registered members' club. This may be important in respect of cinema exhibitions. It is true that the law now makes a number of premises which are not strictly cinemas liable for a cinema licence.

It is a condition of the holding of such a licence that a fire inspection is carried out and there are numerous safety regulations to be complied with.

I should emphasise that these regulations are intended to protect members of the public where they congregate and where risks of fire and consequent heavy loss of human life are at their greatest. But once again clubs which do not show films for 'private gain' to members of the public are exempted, and it may be that your club can qualify for this exemption.

However, one word of caution. Film shows specifically for children, perhaps organised as a 'children's film club' are not included in the exemptions and it may be that under the Cinemas Act 1985 your showings may be classified in this way, even though you are basically a club.

It depends on whether these shows are arranged merely for members' children, or are 'public' in the sense that any children in the area are entitled to join the film club or attend the showings.

There is provision in the Act for organisations such as yours to obtain a certificate from the Home Secretary to make you an 'exempted organisation' for the purpose of showing films to children. Possession of this certificate means that you will not need a cinema licence and may also charge for admission, if you so wish.

Chapter 17
Children and young persons

1 Under-18 problem

Q We have a problem which is causing a great deal of tension in our club. We have a rule restricting full membership of the club to persons over 18, which was originally thought to be required by law. But we also have a family membership system, intended for husbands/wives but so worded that children could also be included. Are they stopped from taking advantage of this by the other rule, and can they use the club in any case?

A It would appear from the wording at present that the restriction on persons under 18 applies to 'full membership' of the club. In the absence of any clarifying statement, I take this to mean membership with voting rights under rule 4(a), that is, your ordinary membership which qualifies the persons for all the privileges of the club, including standing for committee and for office.

Family membership seems to me to be a restricted form of membership, with no voting rights and consequently no right to stand for office in the club. It is only available through a full member, so that if that member is suspended or lapses, those taking advantage of this limited membership will also no longer be permitted in the club.

There is no rule restricting guests or visitors to persons over 18, and therefore it seems to me that you may interpret this restriction as applying *only* to qualifications for full membership, not for admission to the club. Therefore, family members under 18 can use the premises, if you so desire.

I should point out that it is not a legal requirement that persons under 18 should be banned from membership of a registered club such as yours, nor that under 18s ought by law to be forbidden to use the bar area. It is entirely a matter for the club to decide. But members will be bound by the rules of the club, and if these contain a certain restriction it cannot be ignored.

2 Junior members

Q We are a registered club and recently created a junior membership scheme for 16-18 year olds. I say that they are allowed all facilities of the club except drinking and voting. Other committee members think they can't play bingo or gaming machines. Can you clarify this, please?

A   According to your present rules, there is no provision for junior membership. Under rule 3(a), 'Ordinary membership shall be open to all persons over the age of 18 years'. You cannot establish a junior membership *before* making the requisite change in rules.

It is, however, perfectly in order for you to create junior members from the age of 16, and you may curtail certain rights if the club thinks it is appropriate. But you are not obliged to do this by law.

For example, you may accept them as members without voting rights, because the law allows you to 'exclude from voting members below a specified age (not greater than twenty-one)'.

You may prevent them from being supplied with drinks, but you are not obliged to do so. There is nothing illegal in junior members making such transactions in a registered club.

Junior members may play the gaming machines. There is no restriction in the gaming law on persons under 18 in a registered club. However, a club may be refused registration for machines under Part III of the Gaming Act 1968 if the club is frequented 'wholly or mainly' by persons under the age of 18.

Although young persons under 18 are specifically prohibited from taking part in bingo on bingo club premises, this restriction does not apply in the case of bingo played as an activity of a members' club. As club members, they qualify to take part in any activities which are open to them, so it would be quite in order to permit them to play bingo.

What you cannot do is allow junior members to participate and then prohibit or restrict their winnings in some way. Each player must have an equal chance, and to deny some players their rights would be illegal.

However, if you have a rule that no-one under 18 may participate, you would be entitled to refuse a payout to a junior member who unlawfully participated.

3 Junior visitors

Q   Our rules clearly state that membership shall be limited to persons over the age of 18 years. But what is the position of persons under that age being allowed in under our rules as a guest or visitor? Can they be 'signed in' by a member or associate?

A   There is no mention in your rules of a minimum age for visitors. The only restriction which is laid down is in the case of expelled or lapsed members, or rejected applicants or people who have been suspended.

The fact that you have a minimum age for membership may be relevant but of course it is not binding upon you with regard to persons entering the club. Indeed, a recent well-publicised case made it clear that the court had no power to impose an age restriction on a workingmen's club as a condition of registration.

It is clear from the wording of your rule on guests that they are not allowed to purchase drinks in the club, and if they do so they may be immediately removed. The member introducing them may be expelled if this happens, so the stance of the club on the conduct of guests is fairly clear.

My own view is that the admission of under-18s is entirely at the discretion of the committee, who may make a byelaw regulating the matter, or use their judgement as each instance arises.

For example, should the club hold a family day, it would be unreasonable to prevent children of members from attending. But the use of the bar by teenagers might be something which the committee wishes to discourage.

4 Clerk wants under-18 ban

Q I have received a letter from the local clerk to the magistrates with observations on our rules, which we submitted prior to renewal of our registration. Among them is an insistence that we ban persons under 18 from buying drinks in our club. Currently we have quite a few full members between 16 and 18. What happens if we impose such a ban in the club?

A According to a leading appeal case on the subject, the clerk is out of line. As you are a bona fide members' club he cannot insist on such a ban being imposed.

Your rules indicate that you are a genuine members' club operating under a certificate of registration. Nothing in them makes any mention of a minimum age for using the club bar or being on the premises. The supply of drink may therefore legitimately be made to all members of the club, and on their order to guests as well, in accordance with the terms of your registration.

It must be remembered that a registered club is considered in law to be more akin to a member's own house than it is to a public house on a street corner. While the licensing laws may be rightly concerned with allowing unsupervised young people easy and uncontrolled access to drink, the situation within a private club is entirely different.

Persons of any age may not be supplied with drinks unless they are a member or are admitted under the rules of the club. It follows that any person who *is* allowed to pay for drinks in the club, or consume them there, does so with the authority of the club members.

The court, therefore, only has power over certain aspects of the club constitution, to ensure that the club complies with the provisions of the Licensing Act and its schedules. It does not, in law, have power over the admission of persons under 18 and their consumption of intoxicating liquor, which is not, in itself, illegal.

5 Young team member

Q Our club is a member of a number of games leagues which include pubs. The games include darts, dominoes, cribbage and skittles. We have a member who is 16 years of age in our cribbage team and one landlord made it clear to the team captain that he would not allow the youth to play in the league again as he said it was against the law. Can you advise us?

A It seems likely that the landlord has taken objection on licensing grounds, feeling that a person under 18 should not take part in games of this type on his premises. This is an area where the law for pubs and clubs is different.

There is nothing in law to prevent a young person over the age of 14 from being in the bar of licensed premises during permitted hours. Obviously, any person is on the premises at the landlord's behest, but if he has accepted that league matches are played on his premises, he should accept the team members. The young man is not committing any offence under the licensing laws.

But section 7 of the Gaming Act 1968 states that no person under 18 may take part in dominoes and cribbage played for stakes on licensed premises.

If there is any monetary element involved in the games played in your league, or if persons agree to lay stakes on the outcome of games, rather than play them simply for points, it would be technically illegal for the young team member to take part.

You should examine the playing of cribbage and find out if money stakes are laid down. If they are then the landlord would be justified in refusing to let the young man play. Cribbage for small stakes is not in itself illegal, and the restriction on young persons *does not apply* to your own registered club premises.

It should be noted that games of skill, such as darts and skittles, do not come under the same heading of games of chance, and would not be subject to the Gaming Act restrictions at all.

6 Youth behind the bar

Q I recall reading somewhere that only the children of club stewards would be allowed to work behind the bar if they were under age. Our committee has sacked a youth of 17 as a bar helper (not serving drinks) because the brewery said he was under age.

A This is not the case; employment in a members' club which is registered is not confined to the children of the steward. This is only an example to show how the law differs between clubs and public houses.

It is essential to find out, first of all, whether your club operates under a certificate of registration or under a licence, which is renewable annually.

If it is a registered club — as most clubs of your type are — then the rules on children do not apply. A youth of 17 would therefore be allowed to work in the bar — even serving drinks if it was required. Your brewery is referring to the age of persons working in public houses, not clubs.

The other point is that the rules are the same, whether or not the youngster is the child of the steward or other club official. It is a general rule, and there is no specific mention of the steward's immediate family.

The confusion may arise because of the concession for the children of a licensee, who may be in the bar of licensed premises during permitted hours. It has nothing to do with registered clubs.

7 Disco for children

Q I am entertainments secretary of a small sports club. Is it possible for us to run a children's disco in the club concert room for young people under the age of 17? There will only be soft drinks on sale and alcoholic drinks would not be allowed in the concert room even for committee members, who would be in control of the children. Our rules restrict membership of the club to persons over the age of 18.

A As a registered members' club, you are governed by the terms of the Licensing Act 1964 with regard to the supply of intoxicating liquor. But where no sale or *supply* of liquor is involved, then the conduct of the club is a matter for the club rules and common sense.

Strictly speaking, the facilities of a registered club should normally be available only to members and those guests and visitors who are allowed under the rules to be admitted. However, there is nothing to prevent a club from running an independent function at which there is no *supply* of liquor, and nothing illegal in allowing young persons under the age of 18 on the premises in this limited way.

I would suggest that this function be kept entirely distinct and separate from other club activities, and that any means of access between the concert room and the rest of the club where liquor is being served should either be locked or be permanently manned so that none of the children obtain entry.

One other important point: under no circumstances should the young people be allowed to play the club's gaming machines or take part in gaming of any kind on your premises. These facilities should be reserved only for members and guests in the other part of the premises.

It would seem advisable, if this sort of entertainment is to be a regular feature in future, to make adequate provision in your club rules or byelaws to cover the restricted admission of such visitors.

8 Barring children

Q **This is a company social club and for many years we have operated successfully with a variety of activities for our members. Recently, we had cause to contact the clerk to the justices, who informed us that we held a justices' on-licence, not a registration certificate. Does this affect our family evenings and lunchtimes when children are allowed into the club?**

A I am afraid it does, but there is a solution. One of the advantages of registration for clubs such as yours is that the restrictions contained in the Licensing Act about young children do not apply to such premises.

If, as you say, you hold a justices' on-licence, then your bar is treated in exactly the same way as a pub bar. Children under the age of 14 are not allowed in any part of the club where there is 'a bar', which includes any place 'used exclusively or mainly for the sale and consumption of intoxicating liquor'.

However, you may apply for a children's certificate to cover the bar areas of the club. This is obtainable on application to the licensing justices and will permit family members and others under the age of 14 to be present in those bars during the permitted hours.

If you have other rooms in the club where there is no bar as such, but where drinking is permitted, then young children under 14 may be there during the permitted hours anyway, or at any other time when no drinks are being supplied.

Persons under 18, whether they are members or not, would not be allowed to purchase drinks from your bar, or consume drinks bought for them in the bar room or lounge bar. But the law does not prohibit people under 18 from consuming alcoholic drinks in part of the premises which is not a bar.

So in your own club's case, the games room and terrace and the playing fields would be areas of the club where children under 14 would be legally allowed at any time. Once you have obtained a children's certificate, they can freely move throughout the club.

9 Steward's family

Q **We have for the last two years employed a steward with wife to assist. They have two children, aged 13 and 14 who live in the accommodation provided by the club. What is their position as regards entry to the club and being present while drinks are being served and consumed? In**

general, we restrict entry for membership to persons over 18.

A You do not say so in your letter, but from the facts available to me it would appear that your club is operated by a limited company and has a licence as opposed to a registration certificate. This is very important in dealing with a question such as yours.

In registered members' clubs, children may be present as long as they are lawfully admitted, whether drinks are being supplied or consumed or not. There is no restriction on their presence in the bar area, although some clubs do make a house rule that young children should not be brought into bars.

In a licensed club, such as yours, the general rules on prohibition of young children would apply. In the ordinary course of events, no child under the age of 14 should be allowed in the bar of any licensed premises during the permitted hours, unless a children's certificate is in operation. This applies to licensed clubs as much as it does to public houses.

However, there is no offence if the child in question falls into one or other of the following categories:

● Is the licence-holder's child.
● Resides in the premises.
● Is passing through to another part of the premises to which there is no other convenient route.

In the case of your steward's children, one has already reached an age where presence in the bar is not forbidden. The other could well claim immunity under heading 2 above, but not under 1, because as I understand it you hold the licence as the club secretary and the steward is just an employee.

One word of warning, however. You should not allow these children to assist your steward in the running of the bar during the permitted hours. This contravenes section 170 of the Licensing Act, even if they are not paid for the work they do.

10 New rules for serving minors

Q At a recent meeting of local licensees and club owners, we were told of changes in the law on serving young people. Can you explain how this will affect clubs like ours?

A First of all, I must stress that any changes in the law apply only to licensed clubs and not registered members' clubs. What has happened is that in 2001 the law was amended in several ways, to place more responsibility on the licensee and his staff to personally ensure that they do not serve anyone under 18.

In addition, test purchasing has been placed on a legal footing, so that the police and trading standards officers can send young people into licensed premises to see if they will be served.

Clearly, this type of action is less likely in a club situation, but it could happen in, say, a sports club which is frequented by young people, if a report was received that under-18s were being illegally served with alcohol.

The most important change is that 'any person', not just the licensee can be charged with an offence, so that any member of the bar staff can find themselves up in court if they sell drinks to a minor. The law makes it clear that if there is any doubt about age, the server should ask for some form of identity or proof of age. As long as this appears genuine, service may be provided. If any doubt remains, service should be refused.

This does not mean that the licensee can escape personal liability if a member of

QUESTIONS & ANSWERS ON CLUB LAW

staff is charged. The police can still make enquiries about the conduct of the licence holder and may charge him if it appears he turned a blind eye to what was going on.

11 Son helps out

Q The son of our steward, who is 16, helps his father behind the bar on several occasions. Now, it has been reported to the committee as being illegal. This is a workingmen's social club. Is this youngster allowed to help?

A In a members' club such as yours there is nothing technically illegal in a young person of under 18 either working in the bar or dispensing liquor to members, whether or not they are paid for doing this work. This is because the restrictions on employing young persons in a bar *do not apply* in the case of a registered club, which is not considered to be 'licensed premises'.

Under the terms of the Licensing Act 1964, a person under the age of 18 is not permitted to be employed in the bar of licensed premises at any time when it is open for the sale or consumption of intoxicating liquor. The prohibition is general and does not solely involve the selling of drink, but any other 'employment' in the bar.

The relationship with the existing bar staff is immaterial, in the case of registered clubs. The young person may be the child of the steward, or be totally unrelated.

In the case of licensed premises, while the child of the licence-holder is permitted to be in the bar of the licensed premises at any age, he or she may not assist in the work of the bar at all until reaching the age of 18. There is no concession on employment for the licensee's children.

The only restriction on young persons working in a club bar would be in relation to children of school age, where local byelaws will restrict their hours of employment and may effectively prevent such working, where it is known to the local education authority.

12 Banned from marquee?

Q We intend to have a bar marquee at our sports and gala day this month, but one of the committee has claimed that children under 14 must be banned from it, although they may go into the club, where our clubhouse bar will be open as usual. We would welcome your observations on this.

A It depends on the circumstances under which the bar is being run in the marquee. I assume that it is to be available for sales of liquor to members of the public, which your registration certificate does not cover. There are two main possibilities: that the bar is being run under the authority of an occasional licence by a local licensee, or it is being run by the club under an occasional permission.

Because your club normally operates under a certificate of registration, children are permitted access to the premises and to the club bar, by virtue of family membership, or as guests.

The same would not hold true of the marquee if it was being operated under an occasional licence. It would become 'licensed premises' for the duration of the event and for this reason children under 14 would be banned, because it would be considered a 'bar' under section 168 of the Licensing Act 1964.

However, if the club has obtained an occasional permission (*see Chapter 13*) it does not appear that the bar in question becomes 'licensed premises' at all. There are specific prohibitions on sales to, and consumption by, persons under 18, but no reference in the Licensing (Occasional Permissions) Act 1983 to any prohibition on persons under 14.

In such circumstances, children under 14 would be entitled to go anywhere in the area, subject to any restriction imposed by the club committee.

13 Children in night club

Q We have taken to running special dancing and pop-mobility sessions in our club at lunchtimes before the club opens for business. We have now been told we are breaking the law, because under no circumstances are children under 18 allowed in a night club. Several of the people attending are between 14 and 18. How do we stand?

A All licences for clubs have certain conditions attached. They may restrict entry or sales of drink to members and guests; or they may place a limit on numbers. The justices are empowered to insert whatever conditions they think fit for the better running of the club.

They could insert a condition that persons under 18 were not allowed on the premises, and if they did so there would be an element of truth in the information you have been given.

I must stress that this is by no means 'the law'. It may be a condition inserted by justices. But they do not have to do so.

If no such condition has been placed on the licence, then you are permitted to have children over the age of 14 in the bar of the premises during the permitted hours. Outside those hours, you may have children of any age in the premises.

If these dancing sessions are held while the club is, in effect, 'closed' then my view is that the licensing laws are not being broken. A bar is a place used for the service and consumption of liquor. If it is not being sold or consumed, then it does not count as a bar at that time.

You should look at your licence and see if persons under 18 are banned entirely. If they are, then it might be best to go back to the justices and ask for the condition to be modified, so that these young people could continue with their lessons without you fearing the legal consequences.

14 Disco entrants

Q I am not sure of the strict law on this, but where you have a licensed club such as this, and membership is restricted to those over 18, does this apply to guests as well? Some people seem to think that people between 16 and 18 can come in as guests for the dancing, as long as they only buy soft drinks.

A There are two main questions here. Has membership been restricted *by the management* to those over 18, or is this a condition on the licence, imposed by the licensing justices; and secondly, does the condition mention 'membership' or 'entry to the premises'?

In general, there is no condition on a justices' licence that restricts entry to the premises to persons under 18. So this rule would either have to be a house rule, imposed by the proprietor in a bid to curb the possibility of under-age drinking, or it could have been a condition accepted by him at the time of the grant of the licence, as a method of obtaining a drinks licence, in spite of opposition.

The legal position rests entirely on the conditions of the licence. Membership is not by law restricted to over 18s, so it would have to be a special condition. If, therefore, it mentions only membership, then it is a management decision whether they want to risk guests under 18 and the potential hazard for law-abiding bagmen!

15 Son plays machines

Q It has been brought to my attention that during the day when there are no committee members or officials in the club, the 14-year-old son of the steward is constantly playing the jackpot gaming machines. He has won several large payouts, and he is not prevented by his father. There is nothing in the steward's contract about his son being present on club premises. They have a flat connected to the club. What is the legal position?

A As far as I can see, the steward's son has no legal right to play the club machines at all. He is not a member of the club, nor a bona fide guest, nor a visitor to the club premises. He is purely entitled by virtue of his father's employment to occupy the accommodation provided for the family.

Although there is nothing in law to prevent children of this age playing jackpot gaming machines in a registered club, they must first of all be entitled to use the club under the rules. If they are merely members of the public, then the law clearly states that the machines must not be available for play when they have access to the premises.

It is not sufficient to place a notice on the machines 'Members and guests only'. If the premises are open to the public at all, then the machines must be switched off.

This matter is clearly the steward's responsibility. It should be explained to him that his son must not play the club gaming machines and that failure by him to enforce this instruction will be seriously treated by the committee. He is obliged to follow the lawful instructions of the committee and may be dismissed if, after warnings, he does not comply with them.

16 Children in Scotland

Q I have been informed by a friend that the law on children in clubs is different in Scotland, and that many of the concessions which we have do not apply. Is this true?

A Yes, it is. The restrictions on children in registered clubs in Scotland follow very closely the restrictions on children in licensed premises in England and Wales, which do not apply in clubs south of the border.

References in this chapter to the admission of children and the supply of liquor should therefore be read as applying principally to English clubs. In Scotland, no child under the age of 14 is allowed to be in the bar of a registered club during the permitted hours and no one under 18 may be employed in a club if any part of his work involves serving alcoholic liquor to the members.

In addition, liquor must not be sold or supplied to anyone under 18 in the club, and under-18s may not be made members of any club except a sporting or athletic one, or a college or university students' union.

It would appear that children's certificates may not be obtained in respect of the bar of a registered club in Scotland, so as to allow children under 14 to be present for a meal. Clubs would have to rely on the concessions in the law for parts of the premises other than the bar where children may be accommodated, notwithstanding that intoxicating drink may be consumed there.

Chapter 18
Visitors, guests and the public

1 Visitors not automatic

Q We have a snooker team at our club whose captain recently informed me that the law allows their opponents to use the bar without signing in, if they are playing matches. I maintain that under our rules they are visitors and must be signed in and cannot buy drinks. Who is right?

A I have studied your rules and find that there is no reference to this admission of visitors which your snooker captain claims. This means that any entrants to the club must abide by the existing rules with regard to admission. Unless they are members or associate members, they can only be admitted as guests under your present rules.

The rule on guests makes it clear, as it should do, that the introducing member is responsible for his guest's conduct while on club premises and must not allow that guest to make purchases of any kind while in the club.

What your snooker captain has assumed is that the concession outlined in section 49 of the Licensing Act 1964 applies automatically to members of visiting sports team playing matches against the club. It does not. It only allows for the rules themselves to be changed in this respect, subject to a veto on the idea from the magistrates or the police.

Under section 49, if the rules provide for the admission of 'persons other than members and their guests,' then the authority of a licence will not be required for the club to sell liquor directly to them. But such a rule may be blocked by the court if they think it will lead to abuse and indiscriminate sales of drink to non-members.

They cannot veto such a rule if it allows for the sale of intoxicating liquor to members of another club, if:
- the other club is local, and is temporarily closed;
- both clubs exist for learned, educational or political objects of a similar nature;
- both are ex-service clubs (e.g. British Legion);
- both are workingmen's clubs.

You should add to your existing rules one which allows members of visiting sports teams playing bona fide matches against the club to be admitted as 'visitors' for the duration of the match. If such a rule is approved, your opponents will be permitted to enter the club and buy drinks, but their presence should still be signified in some way (*see next question*). The device of making such persons 'temporary members' for the day of their visit is still used, but the *Good Practice Guide* and the magistrates disapprove of it. A section 49 rule is preferable.

2 Two visitors' books

Q One of our members who is also a member of a service club has suggested that we should have two visitors' books — one for guests of members and the other for visitors from other clubs or teams admitted under our rule 9(2). I have always understood that only one book is required. Your opinion would be welcomed.

A I have pointed out before that a visitors' book is not, in fact, a legal requirement for a club. That being said, there must be some way for the club to ascertain who is entering the premises and in what capacity. Otherwise, they could quite rightly be accused of disregarding their own rules concerning the admission of non-members.

Your own rules make it quite clear that the only persons allowed to be admitted to your club are:
1. Full members.
2. Guests of members.
3. Family members.
4. Visitors and visiting teams.

It seems eminently sensible to make a distinction between persons admitted under 2 and 4, for one most important reason. Under your rules, guests may not make any purchases in the club, whereas visitors admitted under rule 9(2) are entitled to use the club bar.

The only difference between these visitors and members of the general public is that the former qualify for entry by virtue of some link with the host club, while the latter may not enter the club at all.

As the people admitted under 2 and 4 above are admitted for different reasons and in different circumstances, the suggestion of your member has a great degree of sense to it. All guests of members can be asked to sign the 'guest book' opposite the name of the introducing member. giving the club a complete check on this class of person. Similarly, all non-members admitted as visitors should be asked to sign the 'visitors' book' which acts as an authority for their visit on that occasion. In the case of visitors admitted under your rules, there is no requirement for them to be 'signed in' individually by a club member.

Many clubs now go to the trouble of having counterfoil books so that a ticket or slip can be handed to the entrant after signing, which can draw attention to his obligations and the conditions under which he enters the club.

Correct procedure of this kind can be a considerable advantage to the club in combating any suggestion of illegal sales and laxity in the admission of non-members.

3 Bingo on Fridays

Q We are a members' club and run weekly bingo sessions on Fridays, to which non-members are admitted on payment of 30p. Can we serve them drinks and can they play the gaming machines?

A Your registration certificate only covers the supply of drinks to members and, on the order of members, to their own genuine guests. If persons are admitted 'on the door' on payment of an entrance charge, they are still members of the public, to whom you are not allowed to sell drinks.

A further difficulty arises in respect of the gaming machines. Machines of the jackpot type, for which your club is registered under Part III of the Gaming Act 1968, may not be used for gaming on the premises 'at any time when the public have access to the premises, whether on payment or otherwise'. This means that on these occasions the machines must be switched off and no one may use them, not even members.

Although it is true that members of the public may take part in the gaming covered by section 41 of the Gaming Act (which includes equal chance gaming such as bingo), such entertainments have strict rules, which again you appear to be infringing. Only *one* payment may be levied, to cover entrance fee and stake money, and this must not exceed £4. You cannot make an entry charge and then allow persons to pay further for cards or games as they wish.

Under this section, any proceeds from the playing of bingo must be devoted to club funds. But if a separate entrance fee is charged, then the bingo must be played in accordance with section 40 and Part I of the Act, which means all stakes must go back as prizes and non-members may not participate.

As things stand, you are breaking the law in too many ways for your own good !

4 Advertising events

Q We have recently moved into new premises and are finding the costs involved are much higher than we anticipated. We have been told that we cannot advertise our events in local newspapers, to attract more people. Is this true?

A It is not true that such advertising is illegal. However, the practice can be taken as an indication of possible illegal entry to the club, in certain circumstances.

Advertisements issued for club events should make it clear that they are restricted to 'members and guests only'. This fact should be stated somewhere in the advertisement, to make the position clear.

You cannot legally open club events to all and sundry, and advertise the fact in your local newspaper. This would mean that you were not operating properly as a members' club, with admission restricted to those persons mentioned in your rules.

Such events would also incur the interest of tax officials, who would seek to claim income tax on the profits derived from public events, as this would constitute trading for profit. The mutual trading among members of the club, including bar supplies, is not taxable in the ordinary course of events.

Some clubs claim that advertisements are placed in a local newspaper as the surest way of reaching their own members and advertising to them, to attract more users of the premises. This is a legitimate argument, and has been accepted in many areas of the country. However, advertising of club facilities does often attract the hostility of local publicans, who consider that it is unfair trading, especially if it suggests that club facilities are for hire or for use by members of the public.

As long as the rules allow, a limited number of functions to which members of the public are admitted, or are permitted the use of facilities, may be held on club premises, as long as the true nature of the club is not affected. The extent to which such a rule is made use of may be scrutinised by the court, which has the power of veto, or of ordering that no change in rules on this point will be effective.

5 Charge for guests

Q **Is it a requirement to make a charge for guests entering this club and can they then purchase drinks?**

A I do not know what conditions were imposed by the justices on the grant of your licence, but it is normal for a club licence to have certain conditions attached limiting sales to persons other than members.

The justices have fairly wide powers to impose conditions on a club licence, the usual one being an interval between application for membership and admission to the club, or a condition restricting sales. You should therefore look to the copy of your licence to see what conditions have been attached by the justices.

As a proprietary club, your licence is renewable every three years. It is more likely that you hold a licence under Section 1 of the Licensing Act (although there is a procedure for club licensing under section 55 of the same Act).

Section 4 gives the justices power to attach conditions to the licence as they think fit. Although the section states that 'no payment may be required' this has been held not to prevent them imposing a condition requiring an entrance fee to be charged. So your licence could have such a condition for guests.

If no such condition has been imposed, it is not necessary to make a charge, and any entrance fee is entirely at your own discretion. But persons admitted must be genuine guests and not members of the public. Failure to abide by this could result in a police raid and several prosecutions.

Again, because you hold a licence, guests may be allowed to purchase drinks if the rules of the club allow, and it is not prohibited by your licence.

6 No payment may be made

Q **We have had a problem about the 'doorman's box'. Are guests under any obligation to make a payment to the club when they are signed in?**

A Your question pinpoints a major problem for clubs which allow too much laxity in their admittance of non-members. You must remember that a members' club is established as a private place, created mainly for the use and enjoyment of those persons who are in membership. It is your own members who may be allowed, subject to the rules of the club, to introduce their own guests on specific occasions.

Your question appears to indicate that this principle may have been forgotten at your club You admit people as 'guests', yet you seem to expect them to pay something for the privilege of using your club. The correct procedure is for the member who introduces the guest to be responsible for them, including making any payment to the club funds which may be appropriate.

Your committee may, of course, fix a charge for entry to the club at certain times and on certain days. If there is a special entertainment, many clubs charge their own members for attending. This is not illegal. But it must be borne in mind that this charge should be levied on members only. If they bring guests, then the member should pay for them.

If you make a direct charge to guests, they cease to be guests and become 'customers', which means that you are running what amounts to a business. The money you receive from them counts as income and therefore profit — quite different from the surplus made by the mutual trading among members.

Although this may be a comparatively small proportion of your turnover, eventually it may arouse the interest of the police and local tax inspectors, who will be aware of the fact that persons are being admitted on payment of money, which means you are trading with non-members. There may also come a time when the matter of a 'voluntary donation' at the door ceases to be a simple gift and becomes, in effect, an entrance charge.

7 Admitting ladies

Q Our club has been 'men-only' for many years. At a recent committee meeting there was agreement to make a new byelaw admitting ladies as guests as long as they are signed in by a member. There were also rule changes with regard to guests. Can the committee act in this way?

A It is clear that the committee is exceeding its powers on this issue, and is in conflict with the rules. The fact that your club only admits male members is an important part of its constitution. A fundamental change such as the one proposed should be discussed at a general meeting of members before any change in practice occurs.

It may well be that there is a feeling that ladies should be admitted to the club. There does not seem at this stage to be any proposal to admit them to membership, but merely to separate them from the other 'guests' admitted under rule 22. But the important point is that rule 22 would have to be changed before this major alteration could take place. There is no provision for a byelaw to over-ride the rules — in fact this is specifically prohibited in the rules themselves.

In your club, guests are limited to four visits a year. The same limitation still applies to ladies, who are admitted as guests. A byelaw cannot change this situation.

The club must take the proposal to amend rule 22, together with the accompanying byelaw, to a special general meeting of members, convened by the secretary in accordance with the rules. If they fail to do this, you should requisition such a meeting, with the required number of signatures, to discuss both their failure and the unconstitutional change in rules.

I am particularly concerned that the committee also seeks in this new rule to allow guests to buy drinks and to provide virtually unlimited access for non-members of the club. Both these provisions may be vetoed by the magistrates and are so framed as to turn the club into a kind of 'free house'. It seems as if your committee is currently pushing the club too far and too fast.

8 Visitors with tickets

Q A dispute has arisen in our club with regard to the admission of guests to functions which are ticket-only. I maintain that any non-members must still sign the visitors' book in addition to showing their ticket. The entertainments secretary says that the possession of the ticket is enough. Who is correct, legally?

Under your rules, persons can only be admitted to enjoy the facilities of the club if they fall into one of three categories: 1. Members of the club; 2. Their bona fide guests; 3. Persons properly admitted as visitors.

It is not clear from your letter whether these 'guests' are really the guests of members, or are visitors attending one of the events mentioned in your rules, or are, in fact, members of the public to whom tickets have been sold.

There is a real danger that you and other clubs are under the mistaken impression that you legalise entry for the public by selling a ticket. This is not the case. You are right to query this admission procedure. The next step could be for tickets to be available 'on the door' to anyone who cares to apply.

This effectively creates a commercial operation which is not sanctioned under your existing rules. If the club is organising such an event, you risk police prosecution for unauthorised sales of drink.

Tickets for club events *cannot* be sold direct to members of the public in this way. Your rules allow persons attending a bona fide sporting event or similar, and members of visiting sports teams playing against the club, to gain admission and be supplied with drinks, under the provision of section 49 of the Licensing Act 1964. However, you cannot 'stretch' this rule for Saturday night dances and socials which are unconnected with such events, unless you have obtained an occasional permission authorising the sales of drink to non-members.

Strictly speaking, if they are guests of a member, the member should purchase the tickets and sign his guests in, as usual. If they are visitors, properly admitted, then it is also advisable for them to sign in, to avoid the suggestion that they are not authorised to enter.

9 Guests of visitors

Q Are certain guests allowed to bring in their own guests as well, once they have been properly signed in by a member? One of our committee says this is allowed under the law, but it does not sound possible to me.

A I think it is likely that your committee man is referring to the facility for visitors admitted under the provisions of section 49 of the Licensing Act 1964 to bring in their own guests. It would be wrong to see this as 'guests of guests', because that is not technically possible, and leads to a form of snowball effect. But guests of visitors are permitted, under certain circumstances.

Section 49 of the Act states that where under the rules of the club, persons *other than* members and their guests are admitted to the premises, intoxicating liquor may be supplied 'to those persons *and their guests* for consumption on the premises as it may be to members and their guests'.

I take this to mean that for the purposes of the supply of intoxicating liquor, lawfully admitted visitors have the same rights as members, and each category is entitled to entertain guests in the same way. But the guests themselves are not permitted to make purchases.

This means, for example, that visiting sports teams may bring their families or supporters with them and they may be entertained in the club by the visitors and liquor may be supplied to them. However, such persons are not entitled to buy liquor from the club bar directly, any more than guests of members are.

Again, this is a matter entirely for the club rules or byelaws. It is not a right. The club takes its own decisions on such matters, and if you decide that visitors may not entertain guests. then that is how it will be.

10 'Good faith' of club

Q Our club is closely connected with a sporting club in the area, to which many of our own members also belong. I asked advice on our rules recently from the local police inspector to allow this club to hold six boxing tournaments a year in our main hall. He said that to allow other organisations the use of our premises removed the 'good faith' element in the club's operation and would not be allowed. What is your view on this? I enclose our club rules.

A This question of operating in good faith as a club has been cropping up more and more recently, and I suspect that some pressure has been brought to bear on the police to curb what is seen as 'outside' activity by clubs.

While I agree that the first principle and objects of a members' club is to operate for the benefit of the members, I do not think that this means 'exclusively'. Clubs often benefit the local community in a variety of ways, and if this argument were taken to its logical conclusion, clubs would be prevented from helping others, because all proceeds would have to go back to the members personally.

There comes a point, of course, at which the outside activities assume too great an importance. If a club regularly hires its hall, has non-members or outside organisations, or even private functions on the premises, it could be argued that it was operating commercially, not as a private members' club.

It is one of the grounds on which the club's certification of registration may be revoked, on application by the police 'that the club is not conducted in good faith as a club'. But the decision in the famous case of *The Little Ship Club* shows that even if the rules allow the club to host functions unconnected with club activities, as long as these are controlled in some way the certificate will not be revoked.

In your own example, I am sure that your rules as currently framed would allow these boxing tournaments, open to sporting club members and their guests. You have a rule which allows certain types of visitors to buy drinks as members of visiting teams or their supporters 'for darts and dominoes matches *or similar events*'.

It might be helpful, for the future, to make your relationship with this club closer, so that their members could be 'associate members' of your own club. This would go a long way to resolve the difficulty entirely.

The police can go back to the magistrates and ask them to impose a restriction on sales of drink to non-members. But they would have to produce some evidence of abuse or laxity to justify this cut-back in your rules after so long.

11 Tea for old folk

Q At our last AGM we passed a resolution to allow retired people, not being members, to use our premises during the afternoon. The bar is closed, the machines are off, and tea-making facilities are provided. It is not our intention to make these people members, temporary or otherwise. What is your view on the legal position?

A Of course, clubs must be very careful when it comes to admitting members of the public to their premises. But I can see nothing wrong in the scheme which has been suggested.

The legal position is that the club must continue to act as a bona fide members' club, which it does. This decision was taken at a meeting of members and the members continue to control the club. There is nothing untoward in that.

You are obviously aware of the main legal requirements. The bar is closed, so that there is no suggestion of drinks being sold to non-members, which would be illegal.

Also, the Gaming Act prohibits the use of gaming machines when the public have access to club premises. These retired people are classified as members of the public, so they would not in any case be allowed to use the machines, although they can be permitted to use other club equipment, such as the billiard tables or dart board.

Nothing in the law says that you must ban members of the public entirely from the premises, but during the permitted hours there is obviously a danger of illegal sales being made to such persons. This scheme is under the supervision and control of the club president and is obviously of real help and benefit to these old people. I think you should go ahead without further anxiety.

12 Guests and machines

Q We have received complaints from certain members that their personal guests are not being allowed to play the gaming machines and are therefore denied their rights in the club. We have always thought that it was against the law for guests to play, but we would like a ruling before we decide on a change of policy.

A I should like to turn your question on its head, by saying first of all that guests in a club do not have 'rights' as such. They are invited persons, relying on the presence of a member who must personally introduce them. They are subject to the rules and byelaws regulating their conduct. It is entirely a matter for the members to decide what they may or may not do while on club premises.

This question, therefore, is really a matter of policy rather than law. If your committee decides to make the machines 'members only' then club members who feel this is unfair may use their rights under the constitution to call a meeting to discuss the matter.

In fact, it is not illegal for guests to play jackpot gaming machines in a registered club. Nothing in the Gaming Act 1968 prohibits bona fide guests from playing such machines and winning the prizes offered.

The only restriction clearly laid down in the Act is that no jackpot machines may be used for gaming at any time when the public have access to the premises. Guests of members are not considered to be members of the public for the purposes of this section.

13 Liability for spilled drink

Q After an incident in our club the other day, I was asked to obtain your opinion about paying for a spilled drink. If a guest accidentally knocks over a member's drink, can he legally pay for a replacement, as he is not permitted under our rules to make purchases from the bar?

A It does not seem to me that this constitutes a purchase from the bar as much as a reimbursement to the member for the loss which he has suffered. The knocking over of the drink, although accidental, was a form of legal 'injury' to the owner of the drink. The action of the guest has deprived him of something which he possessed. He is entitled to ask the person causing the injury to reimburse him.

It may well be that if the offence took place at the bar, the instinctive reaction is to call the bagman to replace the drink. The bagman, as you rightly say, cannot directly serve the guest under your rules, but he can serve the member, accepting as payment the reimbursement which the guest has offered. It's as if the guest handed the money to the member first, and then he handed it on.

I agree that if the guest handed his introducing member money in respect of drinks to be purchased for both of them, that is unlawful under your rules. But this is an entirely different situation.

There is also, perhaps, some obligation under your rules on the introducing member who is 'responsible for his guest's conduct at all times on the club premises'. While this may cover such actions on a strict interpretation of the rules, it is just as reasonable to allow the guest to make amends directly.

14 Hiring club hall in

Q Recently another local club has taken to advertising its function room in a newsletter sent out to its members. It states that members may book the hire of the room on behalf of non-members for weddings, anniversaries, birthdays and the like. We would also like to do this, but first I want to find out if it is legal or not, under Scottish or English law.

A If anything, Scottish law is firmer on this point than English, and such a suggestion, in the form which you have given me, would be _ totally out of order. I think section 107 of the Licensing (Scotland) Act makes it quite clear that members must be *personally* responsible for visitors, that they may only be supplied with liquor on the invitation of the introducing member.

Members could, of course, book a club for their own family celebration, as long as they were responsible for it. But to suggest that a member can be used as an intermediary for other non-members suggests that the club is, in fact, trading and could jeopardise its registration as a result.

This seems particularly so in Scotland, because of the rather stricter controls and tighter wording of the Act.

There is also some doubt whether the device of temporary membership can be utilised with the same ease north of the border to allow other persons to have access to the club facilities. According to Scottish law, temporary membership must be strictly controlled under the rules of the club to persons possessing certain qualifications which must be spelled out in the rules and accepted by the registrar.

I accept that currently this type of advertising has been restricted to members only and therefore has not become common knowledge. But clubs must be extremely wary of offering their own facilities in this way without considering the implications for their registration.

While clubs serve a useful purpose to their local community, they must not embark upon activities which conflict with the terms of their registration or the conditions imposed upon their use of the premises.

15 What rights has a hirer?

Q We hire part of our indoor sporting facilities to a number of local organisations. Recently, one of the officials of such a body became extremely abusive, and I requested him to leave. He claimed that as there was a contract in existence, we could not remove him from the premises as he had a legal right to be there. We would welcome your views on this. I enclose a copy of our club rules.

A Your visitor is quite correct in stating that there was a contract in existence between the club and the hiring organisation. But this does not bring an overriding right for the hirers and all their members to break the rules of the club or abuse the privileges which they have been given.

This is why I usually recommend to clubs that they insert in any agreement of hire a condition that the user organisation shall be responsible for ensuring that their members and guests conduct themselves in accordance with the rules of the club and also are prepared to accept a ruling given by a member of the club committee on any disciplinary matter.

It is an implied condition of any contract of this nature that the users will conduct themselves in such a reasonable fashion as not to cause undue disturbance or distress to members of the club. There is also a condition that users will not break the law or attempt to do so during their visit.

You can rely on such authority for disciplining any visitor, in the same way as you would a member or guest. It is unreasonable to expect the club to put up with such behaviour merely on the basis that such a person is somehow 'protected' by contract, so that he can get away with anything.

You should remember that no contract is merely one-sided and that the persons contracting with your club for the use of the facilities can be made to abide by certain conditions in the same way as you are on other contracts. If they do not do so, then you may seek to compel them in some proper manner, or in extreme circumstances you may consider the contract to have been broken.

Similarly, as the occupiers of premises you are entitled to ask any person who misbehaves to leave those premises, and may even summon the police to help you to eject them, if necessary. This should only be a last resort, as such incidents will be logged and may eventually be used as evidence of misconduct on the club premises.

16 Wheel-clamping in car park

Q We have a considerable problem at this sports club with commuters using our car park during the whole of the day. We want to try and deter them, but are not sure of the law on such things as wheel clamping. Can we put a notice up threatening to clamp cars parked without authority, or by non-users of the club?

A Following an important decision in the Court of Appeal, it is now clear that private clamping of vehicles parked without permission is lawful, as long as strict guidelines are followed.

It is therefore open to the club to seek to deter 'outsiders' parking on its property, but if clamping is to be considered, there are certain important guidelines to follow:

● The notice or notices about the clamping must be clearly visible at all times and prominently displayed at the entrance to the car park.

● The fee proposed for the release of the vehicle must be reasonable and not exorbitant.

● The offending motorist must be able to obtain the release of his vehicle without delay after indicating his willingness to pay. There must therefore be a means of contacting the club or one of its employees at any time when a vehicle is clamped in the car park in order to obtain its immediate release.

The reason for these guidelines is that there is, according to the Court, a fine dividing line between what is reasonable detention of a vehicle and what is not. If the notice is not clear or visible, the motorist cannot be said to consent to the condition about clamping; if the fee is exorbitant, then it could be held to be extortion; if the car cannot be released immediately on payment or offer of payment, then the motorist could sue for damages.

Some clubs or companies use a commercial clamping firm to carry out these procedures, who charge no fee but make their money from the clamping release penalty obtained from motorists. Care must be taken by the club to ensure that the firm is reputable and will comply with the Court of Appeal conditions on clamping. Otherwise the club could find itself in court as well.

In addition, there must be clear rules for who is or is not allowed to park there. Visitors or company reps. could be very annoyed if they were clamped while in the club. Windscreen tickets or stickers may have to be issued to all members. There are complicated issues here and it would be best to have a full discussion in committee and a working plan drawn up before embarking on this course of action.

Chapter 19
Stewards and other staff

1 Need for written statement

Q   I started work in this club as steward in July and have been put on a year's probation. Can you tell me whether I am still entitled to a written contract (which I have not yet got) and what the probation period actually means.

A   There is a tendency for clubs to make their own law when it comes to employing staff. Over the years, it seems to me, clubs have quite wrongly assumed that the 'normal' employment laws do not apply to private members' clubs. Even when a group of businessmen are on the committee, many of whom employ staff in their own workplaces, they still treat stewards and other staff differently.

However, there is nothing illegal is setting a so-called 'probationary' period, because during the first year the employee does not develop any great degree of protection against being dismissed on grounds of competence. It has no real legal significance, because the employment will still be held to commence in July and run continuously throughout the period, and the club cannot remove any employment rights (e.g. by suggesting that the first year does not count towards the period of continuous employment).

More important is the provision to you of a written statement of your terms and conditions of work. You are entitled to rely on this as setting out the basic details of your employment, and you should have received it by now. The fact that you are 'on probation' does not make any difference to this legal requirement.

Within two months of the commencement of employment, the club is required by law to give written particulars of certain essential elements of the employment. They can do this either in a letter, or by means of a list; it does not have to be a formal 'contract' drawn up by a lawyer.

The statement must contain the following details:
- the names of the employer and employee;
- the date when the employment began;
- the job title (some clubs include a general job description as well);
- the scale of pay and the intervals when it is paid (i.e. weekly or monthly);
- any terms and conditions relating to hours of work, rest days and meal breaks;
- overtime rates if applicable;

- holiday entitlement;
- details of sick pay and notification;
- whether there are any pension schemes in operation;
- length of notice required on both sides;
- and, finally, the conditions for disciplinary or grievance procedures.

Such a statement may well contain a reference to the probationary period, but you would be entitled to assume that the employment contract will continue beyond that time if everything is satisfactory and you have shown yourself competent at the job. You are at this stage entitled to insist that this statement should be provided to you without delay.

2 Details for barmaid too

Q **One of my part-time barmaids has insisted that I have to give her a written contract. Up to now I have done everything by word of mouth. Is there any law covering contracts for part-time staff and could I get rid of her anyway if she keeps insisting on making these demands?**

A It is likely that your barmaid is more clued up on current employment law than you are. She does have a right to a written confirmation of her employment, and you could also be in trouble if you sacked her for insisting on it.

Part-timers now have more or less the same rights under EC-prompted legislation as full time staff. They are entitled to at least the National Minimum Wage and can complain if they are treated less favourably than full-time employees in their terms and conditions.

The written details of employment is not the actual contract, and it doesn't have to be complicated. All it has to do is to spell out the basic terms and conditions of her employment with the club, the hours which you have agreed and the rate of pay. These elements can, of course, be changed by agreement after the employment starts, but it is important for her to to have written confirmation of certain terms.

The letter should also give details of such things as days off, meal times, rest days and overtime. You should also include disciplinary procedures and periods of notice to be given.

It isn't just a right for new employees either. If an employee whose employment began before 30 November 1993 requests a statement meeting the requirements described here, it must be provided within two months of when the request is made.

One thing to be borne in mind is that maternity rights have been greatly improved for both full and part-time workers. In fact, this may be one of the reasons why your barmaid needs to be sure of her contract with you, and the date when her employment commenced.

You may find this attention to 'workers' rights' annoying, but it is certainly no reason to contemplate sacking her. You could face a nasty industrial tribunal session if you took such an unfair line.

3 Fidelity bond must be written

Q **We have always run on the principle in this club that our staff should make good any deficiencies found in stock-taking out of their wages. We have not put this in any contract, because until recently our steward was part-time. Now, I am told that there are legal rules for such**

deductions. Can you explain them?

A It has been illegal for a great many years to make any deductions other than statutory ones from the pay of any employee without that person's written consent. You cannot assume that a person employed as a steward or in charge of cash or stock 'understands' that there is such a financial liability involved.

Any question of financial deposits or liability arising in the course of an employment must be put in writing and properly agreed between the parties.

It is accepted practice that any employee who has charge of money or stock within a club may be asked to provide some form of deposit as security against possible deficiencies. This may cover not only the bar steward but also other employees such as a manager or paid secretary.

The method by which the bond is raised is a matter to be decided between the club and the employee. Certainly, any money received by the club in respect of a bond should be held in a separate account which earns interest at the normal rate, so that if everything should prove satisfactory at the end of the employment, the money and interest may be returned to the employee.

It should be made a written condition of the employment that such a bond is to be deposited, and it should be included in any written particulars given to the employee within 13 weeks of the commencement of employment.

I suggest that you take the immediate steps to place these matters in writing in your own club, preferably by arranging a meeting with your steward and any other bonded staff and having them sign documents acknowledging the bond and the conditions under which it may be withheld.

Employment law now lays down certain maximum amounts which may be deducted from wages on account of cash shortages, which may not in any week exceed ten per cent of the gross wage. However, where there is a separate bond, for which written agreement is in operation, any part of that sum may be withheld in respect of deficiencies.

4 Is steward self-employed?

Q It has been suggested to us that in order to get over some of the problems of employment law, we can make our steward self-employed. Can you give us any information on how we can do this, please?

A It would appear from a leading employment tribunal ruling that such a change would not be of much use to you, if the work which the steward does is not fundamentally altered.

The decision will rest more on the nature of the relationship between the club and the steward, rather than anything which appears in writing.

In a recent case, a man had been appointed to the position of bar steward of a football supporters' club 'on a self-employed basis'. There was some discussion about a contract, and indeed one was drawn up, but negotiations were never completed. He was responsible for his social security payment and tax, and his 'wage' was paid gross.

The club dismissed him and he complained of unfair dismissal. Such a claim can only be entertained if the relationship between the parties is that of employer and employee. Eventually the case came before the Employment Appeals Tribunal.

They looked at the circumstances of the work and took these into account in reaching their decision. They considered that, in deciding whether there is a contract of employment or not, the amount of control which the club exercised, the terminology used by the parties and whether the steward used his own equipment were all to be taken into account. The fact that both parties used the term 'self-employed' for tax reasons is not conclusive and should be disregarded.

The main question was whether the man was on his own business, rather than the business of the party for whom the work is being done. If he was asked 'Are you your own boss?' the steward would have to reply honestly, 'No'.

This is, of course, particularly true in a members' club, where it is a legal requirement that the stock of liquor is owned and controlled by the members. It is not possible for the steward to have an arrangement to 'sell' drinks, or to have absolute control of the bar. His employment must be controlled by the committee.

In your own case, with an existing steward, you might also have some difficulty in convincing the Inland Revenue of the change of status, and they might take the same line as the tribunal in this case.

5 Responsible for staff

Q Who is responsible for appointing casual bar staff and also arranging for cover when the steward and his wife are on holiday? Must the club do this, or should the steward engage his own people and be responsible for them?

A The answer to this question depends entirely on the nature of the contract between the club and the steward. However, it is likely that the club will still be treated as 'the employer' in all these situations.

The only time when the steward could be considered the main employer of staff is where a contract was made to give the steward a 'catering package' or similar franchise, so that the club was buying a separate service. In such a case the steward might be considered self-employed for tax purposes.

However, in the normal course of events this cannot happen and the Inland Revenue would consider the steward to be an employed person working for the club and handling the club's own goods.

You may certainly include in the job description or contract that part of the steward's responsibilities is to engage and dismiss auxiliary members of staff. Many employees in other sectors carry out this administrative role.

This does not mean, however, that the steward will be personally responsible for such things as their tax and stamp liability, and that the club can 'wash its hands' of all employer's duties.

In the case of relief cover, this again can be made part of the contract, but it is unlikely to remove the club's overall responsibility. It should be remembered that a stock check must be taken at the start and finish of any period of absence such as annual holiday.

Any obligation to provide cover must be clearly spelled out in writing between the parties, to avoid such confusion in the future.

6 Living near the club

Q When we engaged our present steward, it was on the verbal understanding that he should find accommodation near the club, or at least in the town, so that he would be on hand. In spite of several assurances to us, he has still not moved from his present lodgings, and now the

inevitable has happened during the recent bad weather, when he was cut off, and we had to employ part-time help at considerable expense. Nothing was written down about this. Are we entitled to insist on his moving, or sack him?

A It depends on whether the question of his location was in fact made part of the contract of service which existed between you. It is not necessary that this should be in writing, although it is a legal requirement that written particulars of the employment should be given by the club, within 13 weeks of the commencement of employment.

A great many contracts are expressed verbally. If the condition on location was expressed strongly enough. it may well be considered an essential ingredient of the contract, and therefore enforceable.

You should consider first of all at what stage this question of the steward's accommodation was raised. If it was made clear that the club expected him to move into the town, because of the nature of the job, then in accepting the job he also accepted this condition. If it was expressed more as a hope than an actual request, then he might be justified in considering it as outside the terms of his employment.

7 Rights for all staff?

Q **Do such things as maternity leave and sick leave apply at all in members' clubs, and if they do, is it only the stewardess, or does it cover part-time workers as well?**

A Part-time workers, like their full-time colleagues, are now entitled to enjoy the same work benefits and rights as any full-timer in the club. There have been major changes to the laws covering part-time working in recent years, and they all apply in members' clubs, which are not exempt from the employment laws.

Examples are statutory annual leave, maternity leave, and parental leave rights. Part-time workers should have the same leave entitlements pro rata as their full-time colleagues.

For example, a club worker who works 2 days per week has been with the club for 7 months, when he becomes ill and is absent for two weeks. The club's sick pay scheme entitles staff to full pay on certified sick leave after 6 months' service for up to 1 month of absence. The worker is entitled to receive full pay (i.e. 2 days per week) for the whole of his absence.

Remember too that wages rates must, pro rata, reflect those which apply to full-time employees in the same job. Obviously, the steward or head barman may be on a higher rate, but full and part-time bar staff should be paid on the same basis, and always on or above the National Minimum Wage.

Leaflets and guidance notes on employee rights have vastly improved in recent years. There is also an excellent website covering the employment of part-time staff at http://www.dti.gov.uk/er/. For addresses etc, please see Appendix D.

8 Records for staff on call

Q **We have a number of local people who we call up to work at functions and events within the club, if they are available. Basically, we phone round until we have enough people to work. My question is: with all these new rights for part-time workers, do we have to put these people on the**

payroll and give them contracts, holidays etc?

A In my view these people are truly casual workers and do not have the same employment rights and obligations as part-time employees in the club. The reason for this is in the form of contract which is made. When you phone, these people are entitled to accept or reject your offer of work for that day or evening. They are not required to make themselves available and may simply decline if the timing is unsuitable. They are therefore not on any form of verbal or indeed written contract of employment and are under no obligation to perform duties for the club if they do not wish to.

Although you should clearly keep records of the hours/payments etc for tax purposes, there does not seem to me to be an obligation to treat them as part-time workers for whom employment records should be kept. Again, useful information can be obtained from the sources mentioned in the previous answer.

9 Assistant steward's bond

Q **In the past, we have usually had a husband and wife team who have taken the positions of steward and stewardess and have undertaken as a condition of employment a fidelity bond. Currently, the steward and assistant steward are not related and the committee feels the assistant steward should be bonded as the current steward is. She is reluctant to do this, as she feels that it might make her liable for deficiencies by the steward which were not her fault. Our view is that she ought to be bonded. Your guidance would be appreciated.**

A As a general rule, all persons having some measure of control of the assets of the club ought to be bonded in some way. This includes not only employees, but also the treasurer and secretary where appropriate, and any other officers who handle the club's money.

Bonding does not imply any mistrust of the individual. It is merely a prudent way of clubs ensuring that should be there be a deficiency of some kind, there will be certain funds available to make good the shortfall. I think you should insist that the assistant steward is bonded. This is in the interest of all parties concerned, including the current steward.

However, it is quite possible to reach agreement on the levels and areas of responsibilities for which this bond is taken and it would not be possible to withhold the bond from one party where the fault clearly lay with another. It would be regrettable if the insistence on this fidelity insurance led to the resignation of your assistant steward, but in my view the committee is quite right to pursue the matter.

10 Wife not working

Q **Is there anything in employment law for stewards which states that the wife has to be available for work? My wife has no contract with the club and there is no reference to her in my contract. But the committee are now insisting that she does a share of work, including covering my day off which means we do not have time together. We have been at the club for just over two years.**

A There is nothing contained in the employment regulations which would specifically cover the situation which you describe. If the facts are as you state, your wife does not, at first sight, appear to be party to this employment at all.

Often, clubs seek a steward with spouse to assist, and pay a remuneration which is intended to cover the work of both parties. But any specific arrangement as to hours, and to weekly rest days, should form part of the express agreement between the parties, and should be in a written form. If there is no such written agreement, then the club is acting unilaterally and, it would appear, wrongly, in insisting on these working hours for your wife.

Clearly, you have a grievance which you should in the first instance pursue with the club official who has been made responsible for your employment. If it is the committee, then you should ask to appear before them to state your case. You do not say whether your wife is prepared to work, but if she is, you may obviously seek either a separate contract for her, or an increase in your remuneration, with a variation in your contract to mention her. Your terms and conditions should also be varied where the club requires extra working time or rest-day cover.

If you do not make progress there, then you should contact your local ACAS representative (*see Appendix A*) or the Department of Employment office in your area, who will explain the law to the club and seek to obtain a fair and equitable solution to this problem.

11 Unfair dismissal

Q We were very dissatisfied with our steward and eventually gave him notice. Now we have been visited by an official who says he has complained to an industrial tribunal and there may be a hearing. Where did we go wrong?

A It may be that technically you failed to dismiss your employee in accordance with the rules, and now he is claiming that the dismissal was 'unfair' because of this. Clubs might be forgiven for thinking that there is no such thing as a 'fair dismissal', because of the complexities of this branch of the law.

Briefly, dismissal is fair if you have a valid reason for dismissing the employee (such as dishonesty, incompetence or a breach of the contract of employment) and you give him every opportunity to put his side of the case. You should issue a verbal warning, then a written warning and then finally a written indication that he will be dismissed if matters do not improve. Then, you should summon him to a meeting, ask him for an explanation, and having heard all the evidence you may take the final decision.

Instant dismissal is now virtually impossible. Even where a person is caught 'red-handed' stealing club property, you must give him an opportunity to explain. If that is unsatisfactory, then you may terminate the employment forthwith.

The most important point is to keep a written record of everything that takes place, and put all warnings in writing. You then have evidence in support of your contention that the dismissal was fair.

Employees who are dismissed have nothing to lose by complaining to a tribunal. They are unlikely to suffer financially as a result and may be seen as the 'injured party'. Often it appears as if it is the club, rather than the employee, which is 'on trial'. But accurate records and careful notes will be of great benefit.

12 Committee barmen

Q Because of the difficulty of finding part-time staff, our steward has taken to employing some of the club committee at the going rates. Another member of the committee has queried this practice. Can you advise me?

A I must agree with the committee member who raised the point with you. As it stands, your rule 11 definitely prevents members of the management committee from working as casual bar staff, unless a general meeting of members has consented to it.

The wording of the rule is clear and unambiguous. The work is either a contract or 'an office of salary, profit or remuneration', even though it is only part time. In this context it should be noted that employment laws now apply to virtually all workers, however many hours they work for the club,, so the concept of 'part-time' really has no relevance any more.

In any case, I should have thought that the steward should consult you before embarking on this course of action, because it can create certain administrative difficulties within the club.

As a general rule, employees of a club should not be members as well. From a constitutional point of view, it would mean that they were employing themselves and in the case of a dispute it would be more difficult to resolve.

If you do decide to go ahead with this scheme, you will have to call a general meeting of members to discuss a specific proposal, and ask the meeting for the authority to employ these persons behind the bar.

13 Catering for cash

Q I have the franchise for the catering in this club, which my wife handles. My question is, how does this affect the club for tax purposes and what records should we keep?

A My immediate advice to you is to get in touch with an accountant, who will be in a much better position to advise you. The small fee you will be required to pay (if you choose carefully) will be more than covered by the advice on taxation and records which you will receive.

I assume that you, or you and your wife, are employees of the club. The profit from the sale of food is therefore a separate income, not taxed at source and assessable on you or your wife by the Inland Revenue. If the turnover on food within the club exceeds £55,000 per annum, then you will require to be registered for VAT and keep strict records, making payments on a regular basis.

The club will not necessarily be involved in additional taxation problems, as the mutual trading in the bar is itself not liable to income or corporation tax. As long as there is a properly drawn up franchise agreement for you to provide this service, it would be treated in the same way as any other contract and the club itself would not be liable for VAT returns or payments.

You do have to be extremely careful to ensure that cash and records are kept carefully, both for the sake of the club and yourself. Chaos can result from schemes of this kind which are badly handled, and the committee may become critical unless the whole system is running smoothly.

14 Steward not licensee

Q Our steward has worked in the club for a number of years and has naturally has made friends among the members. From time to time they buy him drinks, which he does not always take immediately, but notes the payment and then takes the drink when he can, which is sometimes after 'time'. I talked to him about this and he said it was quite legal in a members' club, and that the steward had a special concession, like a pub licensee. Is this the case?

A It would be quite wrong to compare the role of a club steward with that of a pub licensee. The legal position of the two is entirely different. and different laws apply to each set of premises. It is often the case that stewards come from the pub trade, and vice versa, and they bring across with them some knowledge of the licensing laws which apply in pubs and then think they apply equally in members' clubs.

While it is natural for a long-serving member of staff to be afforded a special position, he is not a member and has no share in the club stock. If a member buys him a drink, it is as if he was a guest of that member, subject to the rules of the club like any other guest. He must either consume the drink on the spot or treat the payment as a 'tip', which some bar staff do, and remove the money from consideration, or it will cause an error on the till roll.

A club steward does not enjoy the right to entertain 'private friends' at his own expense after time, which is a concession that only applies to the person in charge of licensed premises, not registered clubs.

If the steward resides on the premises, he may be in a position to rely on the 'residents' concession, which allows drinking after time. But this would only apply if the club allowed it. Many clubs have strict rules about the steward's conduct and the law will not act to override the club's directive on such matters.

The matter is one for the club committee to determine, as the employers of staff on behalf of the club. Certainly, no drinks should be supplied to members after the end of permitted hours, and they only have the normal ten minutes to drink up.

15 Order to secretary

Q Our secretary is very upset at the wording of an official document received at the club in respect of one of our employees. It appears that he has been ordered to deduct money from this man's wages by the local council. The letter says that 'Failure to comply is a criminal offence, punishable by a fine.' He questions whether the council has any right to treat him in this way. Can you comment?

A What the secretary has received is known as an 'Attachment of Earnings Order' and it is quite common where a relatively large sum of money has to be paid by an individual as a result of court action.

The most common areas for such an order being made are: failure to pay community charge or council tax and failure to pay maintenance as ordered by the court.

In the example which you have sent to me, the particular employee appears to owe a considerable sum to the local authority in respect of council tax and the council has gone to court to compel him to pay. Because the court believes that he will not pay willingly, they have issued the order for the employer to deduct sums from his wages on a regular basis, until the debt has been satisfied.

The reason for the wording is to give force to the court's award. Clearly, if you fail to comply with any order which the court makes, you are technically in contempt of that court. This would apply in a number of examples, not just an attachment order. There are also other statutory requirements, such as filling in electoral forms or rating requests, which you can be fined for ignoring.

I do not think your secretary should take this personally. The form is addressed to the 'payroll manager' and it is clear that it the the the club which bears the responsibility as the employer, not any individual. He is not named on the form and it is most unlikely that personal liability would accrue. However, the club does have a legal obligation to comply with the order which the court has made and I can see no reason why this should cause any trouble, as long as you explain to the employee why these extra deductions are being made.

16 Safety at work

Q I have just been reading an article about prosecutions for working conditions and would like to ask whether the Safety at Work Act applies to our club. We have four full-time and five part-time staff.

A The correct title is the Health and Safety at Work Act 1974 and its provisions apply to every 'employer', which includes clubs of all types. The duty imposed by the Act is, in general terms, to provide a safe system of work for all employees, and to ensure that the work carried on at the premises does not expose persons to any risk to their health or safety.

The normal activities of a club do not involve such risks as are contained in the second part of that statement. But there can be circumstances in which the club as employer could be held liable for the health and safety of its own employees, if their working conditions were sub-standard.

For example, if the cellar or bar area were not properly maintained, in spite of warnings and complaints, and a member of staff was injured as a result of slipping or tripping, then in addition to a claim made by the individual against the club for damages as a result of the injury, the club may still be liable for criminal proceedings under this Act

This Act does not provide an alternative to action by the injured employee. It provides additional penalties for offences of failing to provide a safe system of work, of failing to issue adequate instructions, or providing training, and of failing to conduct the business safely.

17 Discussing wages

Q A group of our members, who are friendly with the steward, have tabled a motion for discussion and vote at our AGM demanding that the steward should receive an immediate 20 per cent wage increase. We know that this is a put-up job, but what can be done about it?

A Your rules clearly cover this point. Under the heading 'powers and duties of the committee' it states clearly that the appointment of the steward and his conditions of employment are the responsibility of the club committee.

This being the case, it is not the province of the members in general meeting to seek to direct the committee on the matter of the steward's pay. Depending on the circumstances, it might be possible for your chairman to declare such a motion 'out of order', because the motion directly conflicts with the rules. The members have delegated control of such internal affairs to the committee and should allow them to get on with their job.

I also note that it is made clear that members are not to discuss club business with employees. This point should also be raised, because if there has been a move to put pressure on the committee, then it may be that certain disciplinary measures should be taken.

This is not to say that the matter of staff salaries cannot be discussed by the members. But it should be presented in the form of a recommendation, based on sound knowledge of all the factors.

18 Knowing salaries

Q I am the paid secretary of this club and we also employ a steward and bar staff to assist. My question is, can an ordinary member walk in and demand to know the wages of employees? I enclose a copy of our club rules.

A The question of the remuneration of individual employees is mainly a matter for the elected committee of the club, not the individual member. The constitution of a members' club normally vests the responsibility for the day-to-day running of the club's affairs in the hands of the committee.

Each year, a general meeting must be held, to ensure that those affairs have been properly conducted. Accounts should be presented, showing the financial details, including money paid out by way of salaries.

Because of the nature of your type of club, the members do have a right to know financial details. But individual salaries are a matter for the committee to decide. It does not seem appropriate that these should be disclosed to members without good reason. However, if the matter of staff salaries was raised for discussion at the AGM, then they could well be revealed there.

19 Rough treatment

Q I have recently read about a High Court judge warning clubs who employ bouncers. We have two such employees. What is the legal position on door staff employed to keep order?

A Club proprietors must exercise extreme care in employing persons whose job may involve some form of physical assault. The comments from the judge in question came after an incident involving a person with a record of violence who was employed as a 'bouncer'. As a result of an incident, a member of the public was seriously injured. The implication was that clubs who employ such persons without proper checks could themselves be liable to prosecution.

You should recognise that no employee has the right to assault a customer, or to use violence against them unless there are clear and specific reasons. For example, if a person becomes drunk or quarrelsome, then you are entitled to ask them to leave the premises. If they refuse to do so, then you should call the police. In ejecting a person from premises only such force as is reasonably necessary may be used.

In recent years the issue of door supervisors has been taken up both by local authorities and the government. In due course the Private Security Industry Act will require all doormen to be personally licensed, probably through the local authorities, who already run such schemes throughout the country. It will then be an offence to employ any door staff who are not properly licensed.

For the present, you should issue a set of written instructions to such staff, to safeguard your own position. Make it clear in these instructions that they are not employed to use physical aggression and that it should be avoided at all costs. They are there as a deterrent to potential trouble-makers, but the employee must not be given the impression that the management condones or accepts violent conduct.

20 Loss of earnings during closure

Q **My husband and I work as steward/spouse in a golf club. Our agreement was that in return for kitchen and equipment and no rental I could supply various food to members between 10 am and 10 pm, with a slight reduction in hours during the winter. The committee has now decided to modernise the clubhouse and at the same time update the kitchen. I have now been told the kitchen will be closed for 3-4 weeks, completely taking away my source of income. I employ a number of staff who will either lose wages or claim from me for their loss. What can I do?**

A I think you entitled to make a claim from the committee for compensation for loss of earnings during this time. There is clearly a contract between you and the club, to which they would undoubtedly hold you. In return, they are obliged, as your landlords in this instance, to allow you to fulfil the terms of the contract and not to suffer any loss as a result of their actions. Although the renovation of the kitchen will be a benefit to you, it does not in itself outweigh the loss of revenue which you will incur through no fault of your own.

There is also the question of staff to consider. They are all entitled to look to you for their wages during a period when they are available for work and you cannot provide it because of some external factor. You cannot just lay them off at will, and they might seek further advice on the point from the Department of Employment.

I think it needs to be brought home to the committee that they do have legal obligations in this matter. I find that a number of clubs have a very casual approach to employment and contract law in their own premises, thinking that the ordinary law does not affect them. But it does. You are right that they cannot remove a contracted source of income unilaterally and that they should build your compensation into the cost of renovation, as any other commercial company would do in similar circumstances.

21 Days off for barmaid

Q **Our club barmaid has got into the habit of suddenly taking days off at very short notice. When I mentioned this to her she said that she was allowed to take days owed at any time without reference to us. Is this in fact the case?**

A No it isn't, and clubs should carefully check their contracts of employment to ensure that the matter of time off and holidays is fully covered. The conditions under which time off is taken must be mutually agreed between the club and the employee. Clearly, a club cannot function properly without due notice of staff absence (unless there is a good reason, such as sickness). While it is true that in certain circumstances a day off might be allowed in lieu of extra working, or because of a build-up of holiday entitlement, this should be fixed in advance after discussion between the club and the employee.

You should write to this employee, keeping a copy, simply pointing out that in future she is obliged to discuss her days off in advance with you and that wherever possible at least one week's notice should be given. This letter may be important if, for any reason, the employment is terminated at a later date.

22 Complaint over chairman

Q Can you help us with a problem over our bar chairman. He constantly talks to the female employees, including my wife, who is the stewardess, in a filthy manner and makes unpleasant comments. I have complained to the chairman of the club, and other members have also mentioned his behaviour towards ladies in the club. How would I stand if I chose to take legal action against him, or should I take action against the whole committee, who are our employers?

A Sexual harassment at work is being increasingly brought to the attention of the authorities, and you are right to protest at this type of behaviour, which is totally unacceptable.

I take it that you are writing because you and your wife are engaged on the same contract. Otherwise, any complaint would have to emanate directly from your wife, as you own employment would not be affected by this behaviour.

Indeed, it is the responsibility of the whole committee, as your employers, to stop this behaviour at once, or else you would be entitled to complain to an industrial tribunal, as this is clearly an employment issue.

The fact that you work in a private members' club makes no difference. It does not mean that unacceptable behaviour is somehow protected from the law. Recently, several barmaids have successfully brought actions against their employers for constructive unfair dismissal, because they were forced to leave their employment as a result of the treatment given to them.

If your first complaint has not brought an improvement, you should put the matter on a more formal footing and write a letter to the club chairman, stating that the situation has now become intolerable and asking him to take action, or you will take the matter to an industrial tribunal. This should alert him and the other members of the committee to the fact that this is more than just a slight matter of rudeness, but goes to the basis of the employment contract.

Dismissal for asserting employment rights such as this is now actionable, so clubs should be aware that to sack a complaining employee will not make the problem go away. The answer is to deal with the problem!

Chapter 20
Dissolution and winding up

1 Winding-up rule

Q Our sports club rules have not been amended for a number of years and as I have recently taken over I am concerned about the future of the club in its present form. How can we safeguard against the members deciding to sell off all the assets and close the club? Our rules which I enclose, seem silent about this.

A You are right to be concerned about your rules, which seem to me to be hopelessly out of date in several respects. However, it surprises me that there is no rule covering the dissolution of the club, as this has been considered an essential for many years.

I note that your club is neither a limited company nor is registered under the Industrial and Provident Societies Acts or the Friendly Societies Acts. This being the case, the matter for a rule on dissolution is entirely up to the club in general meeting to resolve. The courts will not normally intervene unless they are specifically asked to do so on application by a member or by the committee.

If you wish to prepare a rule about dissolution, you should bear in mind that it should give the whole membership the right to decide on the matter in a special general meeting. It is also best for the rule to stipulate two meetings: the first to resolve on dissolution and the second to decide what should be done with the assets, if this is not provided for in the rules.

The rule should also contain a provision for the secretary to write to every member at his last known address, so that anyone with any interest in the club can have the opportunity to make his opinions known.

The rule should also lay down the majority required for a dissolution resolution (usually three quarters or two thirds of the members present). This ensures that no decision is taken by a small minority.

The necessary changes may be made at your next AGM.

2 Can we disaffiliate?

Q We are an ex-servicemen's club operating under model rules from our headquarters. Each year, our ex-service membership has fallen, and now less than one quarter of our members have voting rights. The role

is now principally that of a village club. Is it possible for us to achieve autonomy?

A It would appear that the only way of bringing about the result you desire is to dissolve the club and immediately re-form under a new name. I do not think that under your present rules you can simply withdraw from your association with the governing body. In any case, as your club is registered under the Industrial and Provident Societies' Act, you have the status of a limited company in certain respects and any change which you make will affect this registration as well.

Because you have adopted the standard model rules, these constitute the club basically as an ex-service club, with objects and membership qualifications relevant to your governing body. To make the change you desire also changes the objects, and as I explained in chapter 1, this changes the basis of the club itself.

It is very unlikely, therefore, that autonomy can be brought about merely by a change in rules. In any event, such a change requires the *prior consent* of the body from which you are trying to disaffiliate, and they are hardly likely to accede in these circumstances. You cannot ignore this rule; it is part of your constitution.

If the necessary consent is not forthcoming, then you must consider dissolution of the club and immediate re-forming. Your rules allow for such a dissolution 'at any time', by the consent in writing of at least three-quarters of the members. There is a complicated legal procedure to be followed, for which you may need the help of a solicitor. It involves the Registrar of Friendly Societies (now the Financial Services Authority), an instrument of dissolution (the contents of which are laid down in the Act), and advertisement of dissolution and various other formal procedures.

Naturally there is a requirement for a final balance sheet, showing all the assets and liabilities of the club. Until this is presented the FSA will not register the instrument of dissolution.

The complication of continuing in your present situation is that you are fast becoming a proprietary club! The proprietors are the full members who own the assets; the 'customers' are the associates and other members who form the majority of users. This is a telling argument for a change in status.

3 Disposal of assets

Q Unfortunately, due to the imminent closure of our factory, the sports and social club is being wound up. We rented the club house from the company and it was a condition of the tenancy that the club would close if they moved. After all outstanding items have been settled and the books audited, we shall have quite a bit of money left. What is the correct procedure? There is no mention of it in our rules.

A How I wish you would send me your rules, then I could see exactly what *is* mentioned in them! As an unincorporated members' club, the *only* thing which gives your club identity is your rule-book and constitution. Without it, I have to use guesswork.

I think it is very sad that your club should have to close, especially as most of the members are being made redundant. I think the first thing your committee should do is to see if the club could be saved, and if it is the wish of the members that it should be.

You say that the company stipulates that the club closes. Perhaps they do, on its

QUESTIONS & ANSWERS ON CLUB LAW

present site; but there is nothing to stop you finding suitable alternative premises to rent, changing the name of the club and continuing to operate, if this is financially viable.

You are legally obliged to consult with every member if your club rules do not cover the question of dissolution or winding-up. You must call a special general meeting and it would seem appropriate to write to every member well in advance, giving the reason for the meeting and any resolution which is proposed.

In fact, the correct procedure is to give the club members as a whole the right to decide what should be done with the funds. In law, the funds belong equally to all the existing members at the time of the resolution for winding-up, and each one is entitled to his or her share in cash. Past members or non-paid up members can have no claim on the assets. They have forfeited their rights by leaving the club.

However, because a sum of money is involved, you should proceed carefully and ensure that each member who is entitled to vote is given the chance of making this irrevocable decision.

But why not try the alternative course first? Approach your brewery supplier for assistance and do your calculations carefully, and you may find that the club can continue in another place, if those who own the assets — the members — decide to carry on.

4 Voting on dissolution

Q Is there any special ways in which voting must be recorded for a dissolution of the club to be legally effective? For example, must it be by postal ballot, or must it be a written vote, rather than a show of hands? What happens if some members claim they were not informed?

A The question of voting on the dissolution of the club should, of course, be fully covered in the club rules, so that the exact procedure may be followed at the time.

Unless the rules so provide (which is often the case with clubs which are registered under the Friendly Societies or Industrial and Provident Societies Acts) it is not necessary to have the written consent of members for dissolution to take effect. Most unincorporated clubs do not make this a stipulation, because of the time and cost involved.

Clearly, on an issue of this importance, every attempt should be made to persuade as many members as possible to attend the special meeting called to take the vote, but in many cases the very reason for the club's demise is the lack of interest being shown. But it is important to check that everyone entitled to a say in the future of the club is on the list of those who will be sent details of this important meeting.

The secretary, or other designated officer, should ensure that a check is made on all members present, so that the required majority (usually two-thirds or three-quarters of the members present and entitled to vote) is obtained. Voting may be by a simple show of hands with tellers appointed to count if necessary. Voting slips for this kind of motion are not really necessary, but a coloured 'eligibility card' of some kind might be helpful.

A claim by one or two members that they were not informed will not invalidate the meeting, if the secretary followed the correct procedure for informing them at their last known address, or in accordance with the club rules. However, the court might intervene if it was shown that by virtue of minimal notification, a majority of members was not advised of the imminent closure and the intention to dissolve.

5 Proprietor closing

Q What is the procedure for a proprietary club with regard to closing down? Is there any legal come-back on the proprietor if the club is forced to close through no fault of his own?

A It depends on the contract between the proprietor and the members, and this really means any rules which the club might have. If the proprietor has limited his liability in some way, then the members may have no claim. Otherwise, they would be entitled to take action if the club was dissolved during the currency of their subscriptions, because the proprietor would have contracted to provide them with services for a specified period of time. In one case, the members were also able to claim damages for the loss of the facilities.

The answer is to provide for dissolution in the rules, reserving the right to close the club to the proprietor, without recompense to the members if necessary.

6 'Hibernating' club

Q Our company has gone through a great many changes in the past 30 years, during which time our social club disappeared for a number of years and lost its headquarters. Now it is being suggested that we resurrect the club, but I should like to know what the legal position is likely to be with regard to any still-existing members?

A Without seeing full details of the circumstances of the club and its demise, it would be difficult to tell you whether the club would be treated in law as still existing or whether at some time it could be taken to be 'lifeless'.

This has been crucial in certain cases concerning company clubs, particularly where considerable assets such as land were involved. If the courts cannot find an existing membership, and therefore no 'owners' of the club, the assets may go to the Crown as what are known as *bona vacantia*.

I am very surprised that some form of winding-up procedure was not at least performed at the insistence of the company when it was revealed what was going to happen.

I think you must make some more enquiries, to discover whether there were any assets at the time the club was closed. You might then be able to discover what happened to them and make some claim from the company for a re-allocation of that proportion to the new club which you set up. If the club has truly died, any existing members are unlikely at this stage to have a legal claim on those assets which would be worth going to court to recover.

Appendix A
Checklist for applications

This checklist is intended as a reference for club officials, to ensure that they remember to renew their licences, certificates and permissions at the correct time. In most cases a fee will be charged, but as they vary widely, according to the circumstances of the permission involved (e.g. thousands of pounds for a casino licence to nothing for a certificate of suitability) and as fees tend to increase on a regular basis, they have not been included here.

Justices' licence (club)

Required for:	Sales of liquor to members
Applies to:	Proprietary clubs
Application to:	Licensing justices
Duration:	Three years (renewable February 2004, 2007 etc.)
Notice required:	Grant: 21 days, renewal: as specified by clerk
Statutory reference:	Licensing Act 1964, s3, s55 and Sch 2

Registration certificate

Required for:	Supply of liquor to members
Applies to:	Genuine members' clubs
Application to:	Local magistrates
Duration:	Up to 10 years
Notice required:	28 days
Statutory reference:	Licensing Act 1964, s39 and Sch 6

Registration certificate (Scotland)

Required for:	Supply of liquor as ancillary service to members
Applies to:	Genuine members' clubs in Scotland
Application to:	Registrar (sheriff clerk)
Duration:	3 years
Notice required:	21 days
Statutory reference:	Licensing (Scotland) Act 1976, ss 102-106

Friendly Society registration

No longer available for members' clubs (see over)

Industrial and Provident Society registration

Required for:	Incorporation of clubs
Applies to:	Workingmen's and other members' clubs
Application to:	Financial Services Authority, Club Section, 25 The North Colonnade, Canary Wharf, London, E14 5HS.
Duration:	Until dissolution or cancellation
Notice required:	On form supplied by FSA
Statutory reference:	Industrial and Provident Societies' Acts

Children's Certificate

Required for:	Children under 14 in bar
Applies to:	Licensed club premises
Application to:	Licensing justices
Duration:	Until surrendered or revoked
Notice required:	21 days
Statutory reference:	Licensing Act 1964, s168A Sch 12A

Gaming licence (Part II)

Required for:	Casino gaming/commercial bingo
Applies to:	Casinos and bingo clubs
Application to:	Betting licensing committee of justices (also prior consent from Gaming Board)
Duration:	One year
Notice required:	To justices' clerk, police, local authority, fire authority, Gaming Board and Customs and Excise (two months for renewal)
Statutory reference:	Gaming Act 1968, s11 and Sch 2

Gaming registration (Part II)

Required for:	Specified games of chance
Applies to:	Members' clubs
Application to:	Betting licensing committee of justices
Duration:	One year (renewal up to 10)
Notice required:	To justices' clerk, police and Customs and Excise (two months for renewal)
Statutory reference:	Gaming Act 1968, s11 and Sch 3

Gaming registration (Part III)

Required for:	Jackpot gaming machines
Applies to:	Members' clubs (and some proprietary clubs)
Application to:	Betting licensing committee of justices
Duration:	Five years
Notice required:	Six weeks for renewal
Statutory reference:	Gaming Act 1968, s30 and Sch 7

Amusement with prizes (AWP) machine permit

Required for:	AWP machines
Applies to:	Licensed premises and clubs (option)
Application to:	Licensing justices
Duration:	Three years
Notice required:	One month for renewal
Statutory reference:	Gaming Act 1968, s34 and Sch 9

Customs and Excise licence

Required for:	Gaming machines
Applies to:	All clubs having dutiable machines
Application to:	Customs and Excise
Duration:	One year
Notice required:	14 days
Statutory reference:	Betting and Gaming Duties Act 1981, s21 and Sch 4

Cinema licence

Required for:	Exhibitions of moving pictures for gain (e.g. video, films and certain machines)
Applies to:	Licensed premises and proprietary clubs
Application to:	Local authority
Duration:	One year
Notice required:	28 days (to authority, fire authority and police)
Statutory reference:	Cinemas Act 1985, s3

Public Entertainment licence (PEL)

Required for:	Public entertainment/special hours certificate
Applies to:	Licensed premises and proprietary clubs
Application to:	Local authority
Duration:	One year
Notice required:	28 days (to authority, fire authority and police)
Statutory reference:	Local Government (Miscellaneous Provisions) Act 1982, s1 and Sch 1, London Government Act 1963, s52 Sch 12

Certificate of suitability (entertainment)

Required for:	Special hours certificate
Applies to:	Registered clubs
Application to:	Local authority
Duration:	At authority's discretion
Notice required:	28 days
Statutory reference:	Licensing Act 1964, s79

Supper hour certificate

Required for:	One hour's additional supply of liquor with meals in evening
Applies to:	Registered and licensed clubs
Application to:	Magistrates' court/licensing justices
Duration:	Until terminated
Notice required:	14 days
Statutory reference:	Licensing Act 1964, ss68-69

Extended hours order

Required for:	Liquor with meals and entertainment until 1.00 a.m.
Applies to:	Registered and licensed clubs
Application to:	Magistrates' court/licensing justices
Duration:	Until terminated
Notice required:	As registration certificate/justices' licence
Statutory reference:	Licensing Act 1964, ss70-73

Special hours certificate

Required for:	Late-night bar/entertainment until 2.00 a.m. (3.00 a.m. in London)
Applies to:	Registered and licensed clubs
Application to:	Magistrates' court/licensing justices
Duration:	Until surrendered or revoked
Notice required:	28 days (registered), 7 days (licensed)
Statutory reference:	Licensing Act 1964, ss77-78ZA

General Order of Exemption

Required for:	Extension of hours on regular basis
Applies to:	Registered and licensed clubs near workplace/market
Application to:	Local magistrates
Duration:	Until revoked
Notice required:	No period specified
Statutory reference:	Licensing Act 1964, s74

Special Order of Exemption (Extension)

Required for:	Extension of hours on special occasions
Applies to:	Registered and licensed clubs
Application to:	Local magistrates (in London, to Police)
Duration:	Varies
Notice required:	One month (written or on personal application)
Statutory reference:	Licensing Act 1964, ss74-75

Occasional permission

Required for:	Sales of liquor to public at special event
Applies to:	Any club or association
Application to:	Licensing justices
Duration:	Up to 24 hours (12 per year)
Notice required:	15 days prior to sessions and at least 21 days prior to event
Statutory reference:	Licensing (Occasional Permissions) Act 1983

Performing Right Society (PRS) licence

Required for:	All performances of music
Applies to:	All types of club
Application to:	Performing Right Society, 29/33 Berners Street, London WI BAA
Duration:	One year
Notice required:	None
Statutory reference:	Copyright, Design and Patents Act 1988

Phonographic Performance Ltd (PPL) licence

Required for:	Records, tapes, juke box and background music
Applies to:	All types of club
Application to:	Phonographic Performance Ltd, 1 Upper James Street, London, W1F 9DE.
Duration:	One year
Notice required:	None
Statutory reference:	Copyright, Design and Patents Act 1988

Video Performance Ltd (VPL) licence

Required for: Music videograms (e.g. pop music videos)
Applies to: All types of club, especially discos
Application to: Video Performance Ltd, 1 Upper James Street, London, W1F 9DE.
Duration: One year
Notice required: None
Statutory reference: Copyright, Design and Patents Act 1988

Lottery registration

Required for: Public sale of lottery tickets
Applies to: Members' clubs (societies)
Application to: Local authority
Duration: One year
Notice required: None
Statutory reference: Lotteries and Amusements Act 1976, s5 and Sch 1

Club rule change

Required for: Any alteration to rules
Applies to: Secretaries of registered clubs
Notification to: Police and clerk of local authority
Duration: Not applicable
Notice required: Within 28 days of alteration
Statutory reference: Licensing Act 1964, s48

NOTE: Registered Friendly and Industrial and Provident Societies will need to complete rule change forms for the FSA, on payment of a fee.

Club permitted hours change

Required for: Change in permitted hours for Christmas Day
Applies to: Registered clubs
Notification to: Clerk to justices
Duration: Not applicable
Notice required: Before new hours are applied
Statutory reference: Licensing Act 1964, s62

NOTE: If Christmas Day permitted hours are contained in the rules, notice must also be sent to the police and clerk of local authority.

Appendix B
Specimen rules

Note: These are rules considered appropriate for a members' social club. Words in square brackets may be amended in accordance with the requirements of the club.

1. Name

The name of the club shall be the XYZ Social Club.

2. Address

The club premises shall be situated at   (state address) or such other address as the club shall in general meeting determine.

3. Objects

The objects of the club are to provide good fellowship, recreation and entertainment for the benefit of the members and to provide premises where refreshments and amenities are available.

Sports clubs may specify particular sports, or recreation in general; political or religious clubs may express particular aims. The nature and scope of the club may be general, but any complete change in objects would not be legally acceptable.

4. Qualifications for membership

Membership of the club shall be open to persons over the age of [18] of both sexes. Membership shall be granted under the following headings:

(a) Full membership;
(b) Associate membership;
(c) Family membership;
(d) Honorary membership.

State here the terms for any classes of membership and conditions if any, for full membership, e.g. employee of a company, member of a political party, type of occupation, Etc.. According to the Licensing Act, a registered members' club should not allow membership other than full membership which is 'significant in proportion to the total membership'. Similarly, restrictions on voting rights must not give a minority of members an 'unfair measure of control' over the affairs of the club.

5. Terms of membership

The subscription for each class of member shall be as fixed by the General Committee from time to time and published in the byelaws. The annual subscription shall be due and payable on election and on [January 1] in each year, except that new members elected during the course of the year shall pay such proportion of annual subscription for that year as the committee shall determine. Annual subscription must be paid on or before [January 31]. The secretary shall post a notice to this effect in the club premises. The club committee may terminate the membership of any person who fails to pay his subscription within the time allowed. Annual subscriptions are not refundable. *Provision may also be made for repayment of arrears in the case of re-election.*

6. Election of members

Every applicant for membership must be nominated by a current member of the club in writing. The name and address of any person proposed for membership must be displayed on the club notice board for at least two days before the election meeting. Any objection by a member to the application must be notified to the committee in writing. The general committee of the club shall have power to accept or refuse any application without stating a reason for refusal. No person may be admitted to membership or to the privileges of membership without an interval of at least two days between his nomination and admission. No applicant who is rejected may re-apply for membership until the expiration of [three months] from the time of his rejection.

7. Conduct of members

If in the opinion of the committee the conduct of any member either inside or outside the club is such as to cause injury to the club's reputation or is against the interests of the members as a whole they may, as they think fit, suspend that person from membership or warn the member as to his future conduct. Where the member is suspended, the secretary shall send notice of the suspension to the home address of the member and shall summon him to attend before the committee to explain his conduct. If the committee, on hearing any evidence that may be called, and after affording the member a fair and honest hearing, decides that the offence is of a serious nature, they may either suspend that member for a period of not less than [3] months or immediately terminate that person's membership. No person whose membership has been terminated may re-apply for membership for a period of [two] years from the date of his expulsion.

8. Admission of guests of members

Members may introduce guests to the club, but not more than [3] guests may be admitted at any one time for one member. The member and his guest must sign the visitors' book kept for the purpose at the entrance to the club. The member must accompany his guest while on club premises and is responsible for ensuring that the rules of the club are strictly observed. No member introducing a guest shall permit his guest to make any purchases of any kind while on club premises. No person whose membership has ceased or been suspended under Rule 5, Rule 6 or Rule 7, shall be admitted as a guest.

9. Admission of visitors

The Club shall admit as visitors members of affiliated clubs or members of visiting sports teams who are playing matches against the club. Such persons shall sign the visitors' book, stating the name of their club or organisation. These visitors may purchase refreshments and intoxicating liquor while on club premises, in accordance with Section 49 of the Licensing Act 1964.
This provision for visitors effectively covers the device of 'temporary

membership' which was used to allow non-members to purchase drinks in a registered club. For details, see Chapter 8.1.

10. Officers

The officers of the club shall consist of a chairman, a secretary and a treasurer, who shall be elected at the annual general meeting of the club. The term of office for each officer shall be [3] years and each officer may be available for re-election.

11. Committee

The affairs of the club shall be managed by an elective committee, which shall consist of the officers of the club and [9] members elected at the annual general meeting. [Three] members of the committee shall be elected each year and their term of office shall be [3] years. Retiring members shall be available for re-election.

This arrangement allows for continuity on the committee and means that each year there will be an opportunity for new members to seek election. A minimum length of club membership, up to two years, can be included as a requirement for nomination for the committee and for officers, who may also retire on a rotation basis. No one may hold office for more than five years without applying for re-election.

If a casual vacancy occurs on the committee by virtue of the death, resignation, suspension or expulsion of a member, then the committee shall have the power to appoint a person from among the club membership to fill that vacancy until the next annual general meeting.

12. Trustees

There shall be not less than two nor more than four trustees, who shall be appointed as necessary by the members at a general meeting, from among the ordinary members of the club. Such a duly-appointed trustee shall hold office at the pleasure of the club, or until such time as he resigns by notice in writing to the committee, or until a resolution to remove him shall be passed at a general meeting of members by a majority comprising two thirds of the members present and entitled to vote. All property of the club shall be vested in the trustees as from time to time appointed, and the trustees shall act in all respects as regards such property, land or investments in strict accordance with the directions of the committee. They shall have power to sell, lease, mortgage or pledge any club property for the purpose of raising or borrowing money for the benefit of the club, in accordance with the committee's directions. The liability of each and every trustee shall be limited to the extent of such funds of the club as may be actually received by him.

13. General Meetings

There shall be an annual general meeting of the club held in the first week of [February] in each year, or as soon as possible thereafter. The purpose of the meeting shall be for the election of officers and members of the committee, the presentation of the accounts and reports from the officers.

Fifteen months must not elapse without a general meeting, under the terms for club registration.

At least one calendar month before the date fixed for the annual general meeting, the secretary shall send notice to all members of the club, stating the date, place and time of the meeting and requesting nominations for vacancies on the committee. Nominations must be received at least seven days before the date set for the meeting. Motions for the agenda, with a proposer and seconder must also be received in writing at least seven days before the meeting. The general committee may summon a general meeting at any time on reasonable notice.

Special General Meeting

A special general meeting must be called by the secretary if required to do so by a requisition signed by not less than [20] members of the club. The meeting shall be held not less than 14 days nor more than 21 days after receipt of the requisition and shall deal only with the business specified in the request.

The number of members stated in this rule must not be more than 30 nor more than one-fifth of the total voting membership.

14. Voting

At a general meeting, the voting shall be confined to full members of the club, each of whom shall have one vote. In the case of a tie, the motion shall be lost (there cannot be a chairman's casting vote). A simple majority shall be sufficient for ordinary motions put to the meeting, but alterations in rules or amendments to the constitution must receive a majority of two-thirds of the members present. Members entitled to vote but not attending such a general meeting shall be bound by the decisions of that meeting.

15. Quorum for General Meeting

The quorum for a general meeting shall be [30] members. No motion shall be put to a meeting attended by fewer than that number. The quorum for the committee of the club shall be [8] members, including the officers.

16. Byelaws

The committee may from time to time make byelaws, not inconsistent with these rules, for the conduct of members and the governing of the affairs of the club. A copy of these byelaws must be made available for inspection on request to any member.

Byelaws should never incorporate matters which should more properly be included in the rules, but they are a much under-employed method of dealing with day-to-day administration without seeking a rule change. Such matters as the use of facilities, conduct of disciplinary hearings, hours of opening etc. can be included in them.

17. Intoxicating liquor

The purchase and supply to members of intoxicating liquor in the club premises shall be under the control of the general committee. They shall keep an account of all purchases and receipts and shall present at the annual general meeting a statement of account from the previous year. Intoxicating liquor shall be supplied on the club premises to members and on their order to guests in accordance with the permitted hours laid down in the Licensing Act 1964 and fixed by the general committee under the byelaws of the club. The hours so fixed shall be posted up in the bar at all times.

The actual permitted hours do not have to be stated in the rules and it is easier to alter them if they are removed to the byelaws for change by the committee when necessary. Only changes in Christmas Day hours need to be notified to the magistrate's clerk.

18. Alteration of rules

The rules of the club may at any time be amended, repealed or replaced by resolution at a general meeting of the club, provided that any resolution concerning these rules must receive a majority of at least two-thirds of the members present and entitled to vote.

19. Dissolution

A motion for the winding-up of the club may be put at a special general meeting called for this purpose, on reasonable notice in writing to all members on the register. At such a meeting, a majority of three-quarters of the members present and entitled to vote shall be required. The assets of the club, after payment of all debts and liabilities, shall be devoted to a purpose designated by the meeting.

Clubs which are limited companies or registered under the Friendly Societies Acts or Industrial and Provident Societies Act have special rules for dissolution (see chapter 20).

The foregoing rules will have to be adapted for particular clubs so as to take in matters essential to their activities. A sports club for example, might wish to include matters concerning playing members, teams, captaincy, use of the sports ground, section activities and the like.

Rules for a proprietary club

Any rules drawn up for a proprietary club are basically the elements of a contract between the proprietor and the individual member. Usually the member signs an application which includes the words 'I agree to be bound by the rules of the club' or similar wording. Although there is no mention of the rules for a proprietary club in the Licensing Act, it is normal for applications for club licences to be accompanied by a set of rules to show the manner in which the premises are to be conducted. The court may insist on a rule covering the admission of persons to membership and a rule on guests.

Other matters which should be covered are the conduct of members while on club premises, expulsion or suspension of membership and payment of subscriptions. If the members are to be given any control in the day-to-day running of the club, then this should also be clearly set out in the rules. It is, of course, quite usual for a proprietary social club to adopt most, if not all, of the rules outlined above for a registered members' club, so as to give a measure of control to the members. Once again, any rules which do form part of the contract between the proprietor and the members must be available on request, though it is not necessary to provide every member with a rule book.

Appendix C
Sample application forms

These forms are intended to give guidance on the type of application required from clubs for the variety of licences, registrations and permissions mentioned in this book. They are by no means comprehensive, but they do provide a framework for club officers which they may use as guidelines for making applications. The words in square brackets indicate alternatives available, and unnecessary words should be struck out.

Application for a registration certificate
[Licensing Act 1964, s.40; Sch 5; Sch 6]

To the magistrates' court for the   of
The   Club

1. I, (name) of (address), the [chairman] [secretary] of the above-named club, make application for the [issue] [renewal] [vacation] of a registration certificate.
2. The objects of the club are
3. The address of the club is
4. A list of the names and addresses of the members is kept at the address given in paragraph 3 above.
5. Under the rules of the club, persons may not be admitted to membership, or be admitted as candidates for membership to any of the privileges of membership, without an interval of at least two days between their nomination or application for membership and their admission, nor may persons becoming members without prior nomination or application be admitted to the privileges of membership without an interval of at least two days between their becoming members and their admission.
6. The club is established and conducted in good faith and has not less than twenty five members.
7. Intoxicating liquor is not supplied, or intended to be supplied, to members on the premises otherwise than by or on behalf of the club.
8. The purchase for the club and the supply by the club of intoxicating liquor (so far as not managed by the club in general meeting or otherwise by the general body of members) is managed by an elective committee as defined in Schedule 7 to the Licensing Act 1964.
9. No arrangements are, or are intended to be made:
    (a) for any person to receive at the expense of the club any commission,

percentage or similar payment on or with reference to purchases of intoxicating liquor by the club; or

(b) for any person directly or indirectly to derive any pecuniary benefit from the supply of intoxicating liquor by or on behalf of the club to members or guests, apart from any benefit accruing to the club as a whole [and apart also from the benefit derived by members indirectly by reason of the supply giving rise to or contributing to a general gain from the carrying on of the club].

10. The club is accordingly qualified to receive a registration certificate [or will be so qualified if, as regards the provisions of rule[s]   of the rules of the club, the court sees fit to give a direction under sub-section (2) of section 42 of the Licensing Act 1964].

11. The names and addresses of the members of the committee having the general management of the affairs of the club [including the purchase for the club and the supply by the club of intoxicating liquor] are [as follows: —] [set out in the document annexed hereto marked 'A'].

[The names and addresses of the members of the committee concerned with the purchase for the club or with the supply by the club of intoxicating liquor are [as follows:—] [set out in the document annexed hereto, marked 'B'].]

Note: the alternatives are provided in cases where there is a sub-committee or wine committee charged with the provision of bar facilities.

The names and addresses of any officers of the club not included in the above-mentioned list or lists of members are as follows:-

12. The [changed in the] rules of the club [since the last application for the issue or renewal of a certificate] are [as follows:-] [set out in the document annexed hereto marked '   '] [There has been no change in the rules of the club since the last application for the issue or renewal of certificate.]

13. The premises for which the [issue] [renewal] [variation of [a] [the] registration certificate is sough consist of   [and are [different from] [additional to] the premises to which the said certificate relates] [have been enlarged since the said certificate was [issued] [last renewed].]

14. The said premises are [to be] occupied by and habitually used for the purposes of the club.

15. The said premises are [to be] opened to members during the following times:—

The hours fixed by or under the rules of the club as the permitted hours are as follows:—

[16. The interest held by or in trust for the club in the premises is   [and the name and address of the person to whom payment is [to be] made of [rent under the lease] [or as the case may be] are as follows:—]

17. Particulars of any property other than the premises referred to in paragraph 13 above which is [to be] used for the purposes of the club and not held by or in trust for the club absolutely, and the name and address of the person to whom payment is [to be] made for the use of that property are [as follows:—] [set out in the document annexed hereto marked ' '].]

[There is no property other than the premises referred to in paragraph 13 above which is or is to be used for the purpose of the club and not held by or in trust for the club absolutely].

18. [Particulars of any] [There is no] liability of the club in respect of the principal or interest of money borrowed by the club or charged on property held by or in trust for the club [and the name and address of the person whom payment is [to be] made on account of that principal or interest are [as follows] [set out in the document annexed hereto marked ' ']].

19. [Particulars of any] [There is no] liability of the club or of a trustee for the club in respect of which any person has given any guarantee or provided any security [an particulars of such guarantee or security and the name and address of the person giving or providing it are [as follows:—] [set out in the document annexed hereto marked ' ']].

In the case of an application for renewal the paragraphs numbered 16 to 19 above may be deleted and the following paragraph substituted:

[16. There have been no changes since the last application by the club for the issue or renewal of a registration certificate in the particulars required by paragraph 6 of Schedule 5 to the Licensing Act 1964] except as [follows [set out in the document annexed hereto marked ' ']].

20. [Particulars of any [There are no premises other than those referred to in paragraph 13 above which have within the past twelve months been occupied and habitually used for the purposes of the club [and the interest held by or in trust for the club in those premises [and the name and address of the person to whom payment was made of [rent under the lease of *as the case may be* are [as follows [set out in the document annexed hereto marked ' ']].

[21. In case any such rent was not paid by the club or the trustees for the club; The name and address of the person by whom the rent referred to in paragraphs 16, 17 or 20 above was paid are as follows:]

[22. The Club is a registered society within the meaning of the Industrial and Provident Societies Act 1965, or the Friendly Societies Act 1974 and 1992.]

Dated the   day of   , 20
[signature of Chairman or Secretary]

Statement to accompany application by club for grant or renewal of certificate of registration in Scotland
[Licensing (Scotland) Act 1976, Schedule 6]

We,   (*hereby state names and qualifications for making statement*) (*where necessary add* and I,   owner of the premises to be occupied [*or* occupied] by the club hereinafter mentioned, hereby certify that to the best of our knowledge and belief the (*name of club*) club designated in the accompanying application is to be (*or, in the case of an application by an existing club,* has been and is to be) continued as a bona fide club, and not mainly for the supply of alcoholic liquor.

[*Signature, date and address of each person certifying to be here inserted*]

Notification of alteration in rules of registered club
[Licensing Act 1964, s.48]

To the [Commissioner of Police for the City of London] [Commissioner of Police of   the Metropolis] [chief constable of   ] and to the [town clerk] [clerk to the [urban] [rural] district council] of The   Club.

In pursuance of section 48 of the Licensing Act 1964, I hereby notify you that the rules of the above-named club were [this day] [on the   day of   last] altered by [substituting for the [said] rules [numbered   ] [adding the [following rules [annexed hereto [*or as the case may require.*]

Dated the   day of   , 20
[signature of secretary]

Notice of application for a justices' licence for a club
[Licensing Act 1964, s.55]

To the clerk to the licensing justices for the licensing district of
To the [Commissioner of Police for the City of London] [Commissioner of Police for the Metropolis] [chief constable of ....]
(in an urban parish) To the clerk to the rating authority for the   of   ]
l(in a borough included in a rural district) To the Town Clerk of the borough of
To the clerk to the rating authority for the rural district of   ]
[(in a rural parish with a parish council) To the clerk to the parish council of   ]
[(in a rural parish without a parish council) To the chairman of the parish meeting of the parish of   ]
To   (the authority discharging in the area where the premises are situated the function of fire authority).
I, (name) of (address), [an officer of the   club nominated for the purpose by or on behalf of the club], having during the past six months carried on the trade or calling of   do hereby give notice that it is my intention to apply at the [general annual licensing meeting] [transfer sessions] for the said [division] [borough] to be held at on the   day of   next for the grant to [the said club in my name] [me] of a justices' licence, authorising me to sell by retail intoxicating liquor of [a [the following] descriptions [namely   ] for consumption either on or off the premises of the [said] club situated at
The said premises are owned by   and it is my intention to apply to the justices to insert in such justices' licence the following conditions (here state conditions applicable to a club concerning admission of members and guests)

Given under my hand this   day of   , 20
[signature of applicant]

Application by a registered club for a certificate
under s.68 of the Licensing Act 1964
[Licensing Act 1964, s.92 (4); Sch. 6]

To the magistrates' court for the   of
I, (name) of (address), hereby apply for a certificate that the magistrates are satisfied that the premises in respect of which the club known as   is registered situated at
in the said   are structurally adapted and bona fide [intended to be] used for the purpose of habitually providing, for the accommodation of persons frequenting the premises, substantial refreshment to which the [sale and] supply of intoxicating liquor is ancillary.

Dated the   day of   , 20
[signature of chairman or secretary]

Application by a registered club for a extended hours order
under s.70 of the Licensing Act 1964
[Licensing Act 1964, ss 70, 72, 92 (4); Sch 6]

To the magistrates' court for the   of
I, (name) of (address), the [chairman] [secretary] of a registered club (a) known as the Club to the premises of which paragraph (b) of section 68 (1) of the Licensing Act 1964, applies and which premises are structurally adapted and bona fide [intended to be] used for the purpose of habitually providing for the accommodation of persons frequenting the premises, musical or other entertainment in addition to substantial

refreshment as required by that section (the [sale and] supply of intoxicating liquor being ancillary to that refreshment and entertainment), hereby apply on behalf of the said club for an order under section 70 of the Licensing Act 1964, as applied by section 72 of the said Act with respect to [the following part of] the said premises [that is to say   ] [limited to the following period[s], that is to say   ] [and] [the following weekdays, that is to say   ].

Dated the   day of   , 20
[signature of chairman or secretary]

Three copies to be lodged with clerk, plus a fourth copy if local authority is not also fire authority

----

Application by a registered club for a special hours certificate
[Licensing Act 1964, s.78; s.92(4); SC 6]

To the magistrates' court for the   of
I, (name) of (address), the [chairman] [secretary] of a registered club known as the   Club, with respect to premises occupied by the club, hereby apply for a certificate that the magistrates are satisfied:
(a) that a certificate of the licensing authority under the statutory regulations for entertainment granted under section 79 of the Licensing Act 1964, is in force for the premise;
(b) that the [premises are] [the following part of the premises, that is to say   is] structurally adapted and bona fide [intended to be] used for the purpose of providing for persons resorting to the premises music and dancing and substantial refreshment to which the supply of intoxicating liquor is ancillary.

Dated the   day of   , 20
[signature of chairman or secretary]

Three copies to be lodged with clerk, plus a fourth copy if local authority is not also fire authority

----

Notice of application for special hours certificate for licensed club
[Licensing (Special Hours Certificate) Rules 1962, r.l]

To the [Commissioner of Police for the City of London] [Commissioner of Police for the Metropolis] [chief constable of ....].
To the clerk to the licensing justices for the   of
I, (name) of (address), hereby give you notice that I intend to apply to the said licensing justices at the [general annual licensing meeting] [transfer sessions] to be held at   on the   day of   next for a special hours certificate under section 77 of the Licensing Act 1964, for [the part mentioned below of the licensed premises situated at
and known as the   Club [that is to say   ].

Dated the   day of   , 20
[signature of applicant or his authorised agent]

Application for registration under Part II of the Gaming Act 1968 of a Members' Club

To the Clerk to the Gaming Licensing Committee for [the petty sessions area of in the county of   ]
I, (name) of (address) hereby apply for the registration under Part II of the Gaming Act 1968 of the club named as follows   in respect of the premises consisting of situated at the following address
The club is a bona fide members' club and is not carried on for any purpose other than those mentioned below. In particular it is not carried on for the private advantage of anyone other than its members generally. It has not less than 25 members and is not of a merely temporary character.
The purposes of the club are as follows
[The club has not previously been registered under Part II of the Act in respect of these or any other premises.] [The club has previously been registered under Part II of the Act. No such registration has been cancelled (otherwise than by relinquishment).
Renewal of such a registration has never been refused.]
I am the [chairman] [secretary] of the club and am duly authorised to make this application on its behalf.
During the currency of the registration, no one will at any time take part in any gaming of any kind on the premises who is not genuinely a member of the club or a guest of a member.

Dated the   of   , 20
[signature]

Application for renewal of registration under Part II of the Gaming Act 1968

To the Clerk to the Gaming Licensing Committee for [the petty sessions area in the county of ....]
I, (name) of (address), hereby apply for the renewal for a period of   *.
years of the registration under Part II of the Gaming Act 1968 of the club or miners'

welfare institute named as follows

in respect of the premises specified in the register and situated at the following address

I am the [chairman] [secretary] of the club and am duly authorised to make this application on its behalf.

During the currency of the registration, no one will at any time take part in any gaming of any kind on the premises who is not genuinely a member of the club or a guest of a member.

Dated the   of   , 20
[signature]

* *not more than ten*

Application for registration under Part III of the Gaming Act 1968 of a Members' Club

To the Clerk to the Gaming Licensing Committee for [the petty sessions area of in the county of   ]

I, (name) of (address) hereby apply for the registration under Part III of the Gaming Act 1968 of the club named as follows in respect of the premises consisting of

situated at the following address

The said premises are not frequented wholly or mainly by persons under eighteen years of age.

(For members' clubs)

The club is a bona fide members' club and is not carried on for the private advantage of anyone other than its members generally. It has not less than 25 members, and is not of a merely temporary character.

(For proprietary clubs)

The activities of the club are carried on for the benefit of the members and the proceeds of the gaming machines are applied in accordance with the instructions of an elected committee. The club has not less than twenty five members and is not of a merely temporary character.

The purposes of the club are as follows

[The club has not previously been registered under Part III of the Act in respect of these or any other premises] [The club has previously been registered under Part III of the Act. No such registration has been cancelled. Renewal of such registration has never been refused.]

I am the [chairman] [secretary] of the club and am duly authorised to make this application on its behalf.

Dated the   day of   , 20
[signature]

Application for renewal of registration under Part III of the Gaming Act 1968

To the Clerk to the Gaming Licensing Committee for [the petty sessions area of

in the county of   ].

I, (name) of (address), hereby apply for the renewal of the registration under Part III of the Gaming Act 1968 of the club known as   in respect of the premises specified in the register kept under paragraph 2 of Schedule 10 to the Act and situated at the following address

I am the [chairman] [secretary] of the club and am duly authorised to make this application on Its behalf.

Dated the   day of   , 20
[signature]

Societies' lotteries — application for registration
[Lotteries and Amusements Act 1976, s.5, Sch 1]

To the   council

I, (name), the [secretary] [chairman] of the   [club], hereby make application for the registration of the [club] as a society for the purposes of section 5 of the Lotteries and Amusements Act 1976.

The [club] is a society within the meaning of subsection (1) of the said section 5, being a society established wholly or mainly for

The [head] office of the said society is situated at

This application is accompanied by the prescribe fee of £

Dated the   day of   , 20
[signature]

Application for the variation of a registration certificate
[Licensing Act 1964, s.49(5), Sch 6, para 1]

To the magistrates' court for the   of
The   Club

I, *A B*, of   , the [chairman] [secretary] of the above-named club, for the premises of which at   a registration certificate under Part II of the Licensing Act 1964, was granted by the said court on the   day of   , 20   , make application for the variation of the said certificate by [imposing] [varying as mentioned below] [revoking] the [following] condition[s] restricting sales of intoxicating liquor on the said premises, that is to say:

Dated the   day of   , 20
[Signature of chairman or secretary]

Three copies of the application must be lodged with the clerk to the justices. This form is not suitable for an application for variations under section 52, in respect of different, additional or enlarged premises

---

Notice of application by a club for a justices' licence
[Licensing Act 1964, s.55]

To the clerk to the licensing justices for the licensing district of
To the [Commissioner of Police for the City of London] [Commissioner of

Police of the Metropolis] [chief constable of   ] [To the town clerk of the [City of London] [London Borough of   I] [To the proper officer of the   district council] *[(in a parish with a parish council)* To the proper officer of the   parish council] *[(in a parish without a parish council)* To the chairman of the parish meeting of the parish of   ] *[(in a community with a community council)* To the proper officer   of the community council]

To   *(the authority discharging in the area where the premises are situated the function of fire authority).*

I, *A B*, now residing at   , an officer of the   club nominated for the purpose by or on behalf of the club, having during the past six months carried on the trade or calling of   , do hereby give notice that it is my intention to apply at the [general annual licensing meeting] [transfer sessions] for the said [division] [borough] to be held at   on the   day of   next for the grant to the said club in my name of a justices' licence, authorising me to sell by retail intoxicating liquor of [all] [the following] descriptions [namely   ,] for consumption either on or off the premises of the said club situated at

The said premises are owned by   and it is my intention to apply to the justices to insert in such justices' licence the following conditions *(here insert any of the conditions set out in form 15, post, with such variations as may be desired)*

Given under my hand this   day of   , 20
[Signature of applicant]

Notice of application for the transfer of a justices' licence held on behalf of a club

To the clerk to the licensing justices for the licensing district of

To the [Commissioner of Police for the City of London] [Commissioner of Police of the Metropolis] [chief constable of   ]

[To the town clerk of the [City of London] [London Borough of   ]]

[To the proper officer of the   district council]

[(in a parish with a parish council) To the proper officer of the   parish council]

[(in a parish without a parish council) To the chairman of the parish meeting of the (parish of   ]

[(in a community with a community council) To the proper officer   of the community council].

To *C D,* of   (*the holder of the licence).*

I, *A B,* of   , an officer of the   club nominated for the purpose by or on behalf of the club, having during the past six months carried on the trade or calling of   , hereby give you notice that it is my intention to make application at the [transfer sessions] [general annual licensing meeting] to be held at   on the day of   next for the transfer to my name of the justices' licence granted to the said club for the sale of intoxicating liquor of [all] [the following] descriptions [[namely   ] by retail for consumption either on or off the premises mentioned below [now] [lately] held by *C D* in respect of the premises of the said club situated at

Given under my hand this   day of   , 20
[Signature of applicant]

Special hours certificate; application for certificate of suitability
[Licensing Act 1964, s.79]

This form may be used in places where the licensing authority under the statutory regulations for music and dancing have not prescribed one for use in their area. As such applications are rare, it is best to check with your local authority's licensing.department.

To the   district council.
To the chief constable of I, *A.B.,* of   , the secretary of a [registered club] [club that it is proposed to register] known as the   Club, do hereby apply for the grant of a certificate by the said council acting as the licensing authority under the statutory regulations for music and dancing that the premises [occupied by the said club] [that it is proposed that the said club shall occupy] situated at   (whether or not they are kept or intended to be kept for dancing, music, or other public entertainment of the like kind) in all other respects fulfil the authority's requirements for the grant of a music and dancing licence.

Dated the   day of   , 20
[Signature of the applicant]

Notice of application for a children's certificate
[Deregulation and Contracting Out Act 1994 and Licensing Act 1964, s.168A and Schedule 12A]

To the clerk to the licensing justices for the licensing district of
To the (Commission of Police for the City of London (Commissioner of Police for the Metropolis) (the Chief Constable of)
I,   of   hereby give you notice that it is my intention to apply at the licensing sessions for the licensing district of   to   be held at   on the   day of   , 20 for the grant of a Children's Certificate under the provisions of section 168A and Schedule 12A of the Licensing Act 1964 in respect of the   Club situated at

Dated the   day of   , 20
[Signature of the applicant or authorised agent]

Appendix D
Useful addresses and contact numbers

ACAS - Advisory, Conciliation and Arbitration Service
Brandon House
180 Borough High Street
London
SE1 1LW
0207 396 5100
www.acas.org.uk

British Institute of Innkeeping (BII)
Wessex House
80 Park Street
Camberley
Surrey GU15 3PT
01276 684449
www.bii.org

Charity Commissioners (Liverpool area & Accounts & Returns)
2nd Floor, 20 Kings Parade
Queen's Dock
Liverpool L3 4DQ
0870 333 0123
www.charitycommission.gov.uk
(also at London and Reading)

Companies House
Crown Way
Cardiff CF14 3UZ
02920 388588
www.companieshouse.gov.uk

Equal Opportunities Commission
Arundale House
Arundale Centre
Manchester M4 3EQ
0845 601 5901
www.eoc.org.uk

Financial Services Authority (FSA)
Clubs Section
25 The North Colonnade
Canary Wharf
London E14 5HS
0207 676 1000
www.fsa.gov.uk

Gaming Board For Great Britain
Berkshire House
168-173 High Holborn
London WC1V 7AA
0207 306 6200
www.gbgb.org.uk

Justices' Clerks Society (for *Good Practice Guide*)
2nd Floor
Port of Liverpool Building
Pier Head
Liverpool L3 1BY
0117 929 7841

Local Government Association (LGA)
Local Government House
Smith Square
London SW1P 3HZ
0207 664 3000
www.lga.gov.uk

Magistrates Association
28 Fitzroy Square
London W1T 6DD
0207 387 2353
www.magistrates-association.org.uk

Performing Right Society (PRS)
29-33 Berners street
London W1T 3AB
0207 580 5544
www.mcps-prs-alliance.co.uk

Phonographic Performance Ltd (PPL)
1 Upper James Street
London W1F 9DE
0207 534 1000
www.ppluk.com

Video Performance Ltd (VPL)
1 Upper James Street
London W1F 9DE
0207 437 0311

Workingmen's Club and Institute Union Ltd (CIU)
253-254 Upper Street
London N1 1RY
0207 226 0221
www.wmciu.org

Index

Dismissal of steward 197
Disorderly conduct 112, 114
Dissolution of club 8, 207-210
Door staff, employing 204
Dormant club 210
Drinking-up time 116, 140
Duty
    bingo licence 143
    gaming licence 142
    gaming machine licence 155, 156

E

Easter, permitted hours 141
Election
    need for 76
    of secretary 72
    required for member 42, 43
    rules as to 43, 73
Elective committee, meaning of 62
Employee
    bonus for 23
    committee member as 201
    not member 45
    trustee as 16
    written statement 194
Employment
    committee responsible for 203
    Door staff 204
    of committee member 201
    of steward's wife 199
    records needed 194, 195, 198
Entertainment 163-171, 176
Entertainment licence 169
Entry into club (see Admission)
Environmental health officer 121
Environmental Protection Act 168
Equal chance gaming 151
Ex officio 17, 58, 63
Expulsion,
    of member 44, 95, 96, 97, 99, 100
    of officer 74
Extensions
    charity function 131
    Christmas 134
    drinking-up time after 140
    entertainment during 167
    guidelines 132
    for shift workers 139
    London area 132
Extraordinary general meeting (see
    Special general meeting)

F

Fidelity bond 195
Fire authority, inspection 18, 110, 171
    limit on numbers 108
Food, for extension 136, 138
Food Safety (General Food
    Hygiene) Regulations 1995 121
Free card for bingo 146
Franchise, for the bar 115
    for catering 201
Friendly Society, meaning of 3
    supply of rules of 39
Friendly Societies Act 89

G

Games of skill not gaming 153
Gaming 142 - 154
Gaming Act 1968 142 - 162, 185
Gaming Board 146, 148, 149, 157, 162
Gaming duty 143
Gaming machines 155 - 162
    duty on 155
    emptying cash from 160
    failure to pay out 157
    guests may play 158
    in proprietary clubs 159
    in separate premises 157
    registration for 155
    registration renewal 156
    separate bank account 158
    steward's son playing 181
    supply of 162
    switching off 159
    types of 161
    use by non-member 158, 161
General meeting 34
    quorum for 79
General order of exemption
    closing during 140
'Good faith' of club 189
Good Friday, permitted hours on 141
Good Practice Guide 105, 109, 132,
    134, 184
Guests
    charge for 186
    children as 174
    conduct of 190
    gaming machines and 190
    ladies as 187
    of visitors 188

Re-election of officers 76
Registered club, meaning of 1, 2
Registrar of Friendly Societies 38, 208
  of clubs in Scotland 11, 191
Registration certificate
  cancellation of 10
  for gaming 142
  for gaming machines 142, 155
  for lottery 149
  not for licensed premises 10
  qualifications for 2, 3, 5
  renewal for machines 156
  renewal of 56, 57, 113, 175
  surrender of 7
  variation of 107
Registration under Gaming Act Part III 9
Regular extension (Scotland) 129
Requisition, for special meeting 85
  not quorum 86
Renovation of club 19
Resolution, at special general meeting 91
Restaurant
  extensions for 137
  licence for 9
Rights of members (see members)
Rules 33-40
  alteration of 35, 109
  amendment of 35
  as contract 33
  conflict in 36
  copy of 39
  enforcement of 41
  essential 33
  for bingo 144
  for election 42
  for proprietary club 40
  illegal change of 84
  interpretation of 37, 71
  note of changes in 37
  notifying changes of 38, 107
  on children 177
  on dissolution 207
  opening times on 40
  reprinting 34
  standing orders and 37
  trustees on 12
  visitors on 183

S

Sale of intoxicating liquor
  in registered club 115, 120
Sandwiches, not a meal 136
Scotland, children in 181
  registration in 10, 113, 129
  hiring club in 192
Schedule 7, meaning of 5
Secretary
  as permanent post 72
  duties of 51, 54, 56, 202
  election of 72
  entertaining friends 129
  notifying clerk 127
  notifying name of 56
  not licensee 55
  power over staff 55
  salary for 54, 58
  standing in for 57
  trustee as 15
  voting rights of 58
Self-employed, definition of 196
Servicemens club, disaffiliation 8, 207
Sex Discrimination Act 1975 49
Smoking, by bar staff 121
Snooker, not gaming 153
Snowball prize at bingo 144, 147
Special occasion , other premises on 124
Special general meeting 83, 84, 86, 89, 91
Special hours certificate 111, 137
Special order of exemption 139, 140
Speeches, at meetings 80
Spilling a drink 190
Staff
  authority over 55
  drinks after time 130
  employment of 197
  holidays for 205
  Inland Revenue and 196, 197, 201
  instructions to 205
  maternity rights for 198
  not members 201
  on call 198
  safety at work of 203
  seeing wages of 204
  sexual harassment 206
  sick pay for 198
  single minimum rate for 195
  tax on pay of 196, 197

Under 18 176
written statement for 194, 195
Standing orders 37
Statutory Sick Pay 198
Steward
accommodation of 197
as chairman 67
appointing staff 197
bond for assistant 199
catering by wife of 201
child of, working 178, 179
children of, in club 177
contract for 194
dismissal of 200
fidelity bond for 195
in proprietary club 177
liability in law of 116
members obey instruction of 102
not licensee 202
on committee 67
powers of 102
self-employed 196
spouse of, assisting 199
stock deficiencies and 24
Sub-committee, secretary on 58
Subscription
arrears of 46
late payment of 47
long-term 43
not returnable 45
waiving 46
Sunday, dancing on 170
Sunday Entertainments Act 1932 170
Supper hour certificate 136, 137, 138
Supplier, change of 85
Surplus, members' club trading 21
Suspension of member 75, 100

T

Tea, for old folk 189
Television 164
Temporary membership 48, 101
Temporary premises, supply of drink
on 123
Tickets
admission 187
for bingo 146
lottery 147
numbered 171
separate winning 149
unclaimed tote 148
Trade Descriptions Act 1968 122, 138

Treasurer
duties of 53
presenting accounts 25
removal of 59
Trustee Act 1925 12, 14
Trustee
appointment of 12
as employee 16
at sub-committee 17
death of 13
financial liability of 13
power of 17
refusing to sign 14
removal of 16
rules on 12
under Friendly Societies Act 13

U

Unfair dismissal 58, 200

V

Valued Added Tax 23, 154, 201
Video films 166
Videograms, meaning of 166
Video Performance Ltd (VPL) 167
Visiting teams 183, 184, 189
Visitors 183 - 188
admission of 183
buying drinks 184
children as 174
guests of 188
signing in of 183, 184, 188
with tickets 187
Visitors' book 184, 188
Voting
as chairman 90
at annual general meeting 92, 93
by committee 93
contrary to rule book 83
eligibility 92, 93
in committee 64
in general meeting 34, 62
majority 91
methods of 82, 209
on dissolution 209
on secretary's salary 58
on suspended member 99
order of 76
persons under 21 77
proxy 90

Notes